HOW TO

Pull a Bloke

in

Seven

Languages

This is a Carlton Book

Text and design copyright © 1998 Carlton Books

This edition published by Carlton Books Limited 1998

ISBN 1 85868 407 2

Printed and bound in Great Britain

HOW TO

Pull a Bloke

in Seven Languages

The ultimate guide to success with men from around the world

CARLTON

Girl power has finally come of age with this fantastic collection of chat-up lines. No matter what the occasion, there's a witty, sexy or romantic one-liner that will break the ice in the way you want. When it's time to dazzle the lucky guy you've set your eye on, you'll have the right words to impress him right here at your fingertips. Translations are provided, so the language barrier will prove no problem when you want to snare that holiday hunk. In fact, the lines in this book make dating so easy, it's almost unfair!

Contents

Chat-up lines for...

Chat-up lines that are...

Anywhere...

Anywhere...

GB "Didn't we go to different schools together?"

F « Ne sommes-nous pas allés ensemble à des écoles différentes ? »

D „Waren wir nicht gleichzeitig auf verschiedenen Schulen ? "

I "Non eravamo insieme in classi diverse?"

E "¿No fuimos juntos a distintos colegios?"

P "Não estivemos em escolas diferentes juntos?"

S "Gick inte vi på olika skolor tillsammans?"

Anywhere...

GB "I think what we have here is a meaningful flirtation."

F «Voilà un flirt qui en dit long.»

D „Ich glaube, dies ist ein typischer Fall von einem bedeutenden Flirt."

I "Credo che quello che sta nascendo in questo momento tra noi diventerai una scappatella densa di significati."

E "Creo que lo que tenemos aquí es un ligue muy serio."

P "Penso que o que temos aqui é um namorico significativo.`"

S "Jag tror att vi har någonting på gång."

Anywhere...

GB "Come on, you'll do."

F « Allez, ça ira, tu feras l'affaire. »

D „Kommen Sie, Sie sind gut genug."

I "Ma sì, tu mi vai bene."

E "Vamos, me quedo contigo."

P "Vamos, você serve."

S "Kom igen, du får duga."

GB
"Hi, I'm new here. Could you show me to your favourite restaurant?"

F
« Salut ! Je suis nouvelle ici. Pouvez-vous me montrer votre restaurant préféré ? »

D
„ Hallo, ich bin neu hier, können Sie mich zu Ihrem Lieblingsrestaurant bringen ? "

I
"Ciao, sono nuova da queste parti. Potresti portarmi dal tuo ristorante preferito?"

E
"Hola. Soy nueva aquí. ¿Me enseñas tu restaurante favorito?"

P
"Olá, sou nova aqui. Podia indicar-me o seu restaurante favorito?"

S
"Hej, jag är ny här. Kan du visa mig vägen till din favoritrestaurang?"

Anywhere...

GB [Write on a card] "Smile if you want to go to bed with me."

F [A écrire sur une carte] «Souris si tu veux coucher avec moi.»

D (Auf eine Karte schreiben) „Lächeln Sie bitte, wenn Sie mit mir ins Bett wollen. "

I [Scrivi su un biglietto] "Sorridi se vuoi venire a letto con me."

E [Escribe en una tarjeta] "Sonríe si quieres acostarte conmigo."

P [Escrito num cartão] "Sorria se quiser ir para a cama comigo."

S [Skriv på ett kort:] "Le om du vill gå till sängs med mig."

Anywhere...

GB "Until I saw you, I knew I only fancied other girls. Now I'm confused. Help me?"

F «Avant de te rencontrer je ne m'intéressait qu'aux filles. Aujourd'hui je suis perdue. A l'aide!»

D „Bis ich Sie sah, habe ich mich nur in andere Frauen verliebt. Jetzt bin ich ganz durcheinander. Können Sie mir helfen?"

I "Prima di vederti, ero sicura di essere attratta solamente da altre donne. Ma ora sono confusa. Mi vuoi aiutare?"

E "Hasta que te he visto creía que sólo me gustaban las chicas. Ahora estoy confundida. ¿Me ayudas?"

P "Até ao momento em que o vi, pensava que apenas gostava de outras mulheres. Agora estou confusa. Ajuda-me?"

S "Jag var lesbisk tills jag såg dig."

Anywhere...

GB   "Do you have a girlfriend? Wouldn't you like a second one for special occasions?"

F   « As-tu une petite amie ? Ça te dirait d'en avoir une autre pour les occasions spéciales ? »

D   „ Haben Sie eine Freundin ? Vielleicht brauchen Sie eine Zweite für besondere Gelegenheiten ? "

I   "Hai la ragazza? Non ti piacerebbe averne un'altra per le occasioni speciali?"

E   "¿Tienes novia? ¿Te gustaría tener una más para ocasiones especiales?"

P   "Tem uma namorada? Não gostaria de ter uma segunda para ocasiões especiais?"

S   "Har du flickvän? Du skulle inte vilja ha en till för speciella tillfällen?"

Anywhere...

GB "Hey baby, want to get lucky?"

F « Hé chéri, tu veux tenter ta chance? »

D „ Hi Baby, wollen Sie Glück haben ? "

I "Ciao bello, vuoi vedere se hai fortuna con me?"

E "Oye guapo ¿te hago un favor?"

P "Oi, jeitoso, queres ser um felizardo?"

S "Hej snygging, vill du bli lycklig?"

Anywhere...

GB "Hi, 1 just noticed you looking at me across the room. I'll give a minute to catch your breath."

F « Salut ! J'ai vu que tu me regardais depuis l'autre côté de la salle. Je te donne une minute pour retenir ton souffle »

D „ Hallo, ich habe gerade gesehen, dass Sie mich da drüben gesehen haben. Ich gebe Ihnen eine Minute wieder Luft zu bekommen. "

I "Ciao, ho notato che mi stavi guardando. Ti concedo un minuto per riprendere fiato."

E "Hola. Acabo de darme cuenta de que me mirabas desde la otra punta de la sala. Te daré un minuto para que recuperes la respiración."

P "Olá, acabo de reparar que estavas a olhar para mim do outro lado da sala. Dou-te um minuto para recuperares a respiração."

S "Hej, jag märkte att du tittade på mig från andra sidan rummet. Behöver du hämta andan?"

GB "I can tell that your body is really lonely."

F « Je constate que ton corps est terriblement seul. »

D „Ich kann deutlich sehen, dass Ihr Körper schrecklich allein ist. "

I "Posso indovinare che il tuo corpo si sente terribilmente solo."

E "Se nota que tu cuerpo está muy solo."

P "Posso dizer-lhe que o seu corpo está verdadeiramente solitário."

S "Jag ser att din kropp är väldigt ensam."

Anywhere...

GB "If I gave you my phone number, would you keep it or throw it away?"

F « Si je te donne mon numéro de téléphone, tu le gardes ou tu le jettes? »

D „Wenn ich Ihnen meine Telefonnummer gäbe,würden Sie sie wegwerfen oder behalten ? "

I "Se ti dò il mio numero di telefono, lo usi o lo getti via?"

E "Si te diera mi número de teléfono ¿te lo guardarías o lo tirarías?"

P "Se eu lhe der o meu número de telefone, vai guardá-lo ou deitá-lo fora?"

S "Om jag gav dig mitt telefonnummer, skulle du behålla eller kasta det?"

Anwhere...

GB [As he walks past, follow and say:] "So, where are we going?"

F [Il passe, le suivre et dire :] «Alors où allons-nous comme ça?»

D (Während er vorbei geht, folgen Sie ihm und sagen): „So, wo gehen wir denn hin?"

I [Quando ti passa vicino, seguilo e digli:] "Allora, dove stiamo andando?"

E [Cuando pase por delante, síguelo y dile:] "Bueno ¿a dónde vamos?"

P [Quando ele passa, segue-o e diz:] "Então, onde é que vamos?"

S [När han går förbi, följ efter och säg:] "Vart är vi på väg?"

Anywhere...

GB "Hi. My name is [your name]. How do you like me so far?"

F «Salut ! Je m'appelle [votre nom]. Ça te plaît jusque là ? »

D „Hallo, mein Name ist (Ihr Name). Wie gefalle ich Ihnen bis jetzt ? "

I "Ciao. Mi chiamo [il tuo nome]. Quanto ti piaccio?"

E "Hola. Me llamo [tu nombre].¿Qué te he parecido hasta ahora?"

P "Olá. O meu nome é [o nome]. Como me achaste até agora?"

S "Hej. Jag heter [ditt namn]. Vad tycker du om mig hittills?"

GB "I saw you at the party last weekend and you look interesting... Let's meet sometime."

F «Je t'ai vu à la fête le week-end dernier et tu me semble intéressant...on pourrait se revoir un jour?»

D „Ich sah Sie letzte Woche auf einer Party und Sie schienen interessant... Wir müssen uns irgendwann treffen. "

I "Ti ho visto ad una festa alcuni giorni fa e mi sei sembrato interessante... perchè non ci vediamo qualche volta?"

E "Te vi en la fiesta el fin de semana pasado y me pareciste interesante... Salgamos juntos alguna vez."

P "Vi-te na festa da semana passada e pareceste-me interessante... Vamo-nos conhecer qualquer dia."

S "Jag såg dig på festen förra helgen och du ser intressant ut... Vi kan väl träffas någon gång."

Anywhere...

GB "Mmmm, you bring new meaning to the word 'edible'."

F « Miam, miam, on en mangerait ! »

D „ Mhhh, Sie geben dem Begriff „„ eßbar "" eine neue Bedeutung. "

I "Hmmm, dai un significato nuovo alla parola 'commestibile'."

E "Mmmm, has dado un nuevo significado a la palabra 'comestible'."

P "Mmmm, tu dás um novo significado à palavra 'comestível'."

S "Mmmm, du ger ordet 'ätbar' en helt ny mening."

Anywhere...

GB [Write on a card] "Believe me when I say that my heart cries out to you and if kisses could be sent in writing you would be reading this note with your lips."

F [Écrire sur une carte] « Croyez moi quand je vous dit que mon cœur vous appelle et que si les baisers pouvaient s'écrire, vous liriez ces lignes de vos lèvres. »

D (Auf eine Karte schreiben) „Glauben Sie mir, wenn ich Ihnen sag, dass mein Herz nach Ihnen ruft und wenn es Küsse schicken könnte, würden Sie diesen Zettel mit Ihren Lippen lesen. "

I [Scrivi su un biglietto] "Credimi quando ti dico che il mio cuore ti desidera e che se fosse possibile mandare baci per lettera, queste parole le leggeresti con le tue labbra."

E [Escribe en una tarjeta] "Créeme si te digo que mi corazón te pide a gritos. Si los besos pudieran enviarse por escrito, estarías leyendo esta nota con los labios."

P [Escrito num cartão] "Acredite em mim, quando digo que o meu corção palpita por si e se fosse possível enviar beijos por escrito você estaria a ler esta carta com os lábios."

S [Skriv på ett kort] "Tro mig när jag säger att mitt hjärta skriker efter dig och att om kyssar kunde ges i skrift skulle du läsa det här kortet med dina läppar."

Anywhere...

GB "Your hair would look wonderful with my fingers running through it."

F « Tes cheveux seraient plus beaux si je pouvais y passer la main »

D „ Ihr Haar würde gut aussehen, wenn meine Finger dadurch fahren. "

I "Sono sicura che se facessi passare le mie dita tra i tuoi capelli, sarebbero ancora più meravigliosi."

E "Tu pelo estaría precioso enredado en mis dedos."

P "O teu cabelo ficaria maravilhoso com os meus dedos a acariciá-lo."

S "Ditt hår skulle se underbart ut på min kudde."

Anywhere...

GB "Pardon me, is your seat taken?

F « Excusez-moi, est ce que votre place est occupée? »

D „ Entschuldigung, ist Ihr Stuhl besetzt ? "

I "Mi scusi, ma è occupato il suo posto?"

E "Perdona ¿está ocupado tu asiento?"

P "Desculpe, este lugar está ocupado?"

S "Ursäkta mig, är din stol upptagen?"

Anywhere...

GB "So, what are the chances that we can engage in anything more than just conversation?"

F « Quelles sont nos chances d'engager plus qu'une conversation ? »

D „ So, wie stehen die Aussichten, dass wir in mehr als eine angenehme Unterhaltung verwickelt werden ? "

I "Allora, che possibilità ho di avere qualcosa di più di una conversazione con te?"

E "Así que ¿qué posibilidades tenemos de enrollarnos en algo más que una conversación?"

P "Enão, quais são as hipóteses de nos comprometermos em algo mais do que conversa?"

S "Kan vi inte ägna oss åt något annat än bara konversation?"

The Bar...

The Bar...

GB "Be unique. Be different. Buy me a drink."

F « Soyez unique, soyez différent. Offrez moi un verre »

D „ Seien Sie anders, Seien Sie etwas Besonders, geben Sie mir einen aus. "

I "Fai l'originale. Fai il diverso. Offrimi da bere."

E "Sé único. Sé diferente. Invítame a una copa."

P "Sê único. Sê diferente. Oferece-me uma bebida."

S "Var unik. Var annorlunda. Bjud mig på en drink."

GB "Forgive me if I babble, but I'm terrified I may never get to know you. Please will you buy me a drink to steady my nerves?"

F « Excusez-moi si je bredouille mais j'ai très peur de ne jamais pouvoir vous connaître. Vous voulez bien m'offrir un verre pour que je me calme ? »

D „Entschuldigen Sie, wenn ich Blödsinn rede, aber ich habe solche Angst, dass wir uns niemals richtig kennenlernen. Können Sie mir bitte einen ausgeben, damit ich mich beruhigen kann ? "

I "Perdonami se sto farfugliando, ma ho il terrore che non riuscirò mai a conoscerti. Offrimi da bere per calmarmi i nervi, per piacere."

E "Perdóname si balbuceo, pero me aterra pensar que nunca te pueda llegar a conocer. Por favor, invítame a una copa para calmarme los nervios."

P "Perdoe-me por estar a balbuciar, mas aterroriza-me pensar que poderia nunca vir a conhecê-lo. Oferece-me uma bebida para acalmar os nervos?"

S "Ursäkta mig om jag pladdrar på, men jag är livrädd att jag aldrig kommer att lära känna dig. Snälla, du kan väl bjuda mig på en drink för att lugna min nerver?"

The Bar...

GB "Hi. I suffer from amnesia. Do I come here often?"

F « Salut ! Je suis amnésique. Est-ce que je viens ici souvent ? »

D „Hallo, ich leide an Amnesie. Bin ich hier oft ? "

I "Ciao. Soffro di amnesia. Vengo spesso in questo bar?"

E "Hola. Sufro amnesia. ¿Vengo por aquí a menudo?"

P "Olá. Sofro de amanésia. Costumo vir aqui muitas vezes?"

S "Hej, jag lider av minnesförlust. Brukar jag komma hit ofta?"

GB "Hi, can 1 buy you several drinks?"

F « Salut ! Est-ce que je peux vous offrir plusieurs verres ? »

D „ Hallo, kann ich Ihnen mehrere ausgeben ? "

I "Ciao, posso offrirti da bere molte volte?"

E "Hola ¿puedo invitarte a varias copas?"

P "Olá, posso oferecer-lhe várias bebidas?"

S "Hej, får jag bjuda på flera drinkar?"

The Bar...

GB "Hi, we're taking a survey and I need your phone number. If you give it to me, I'll call you and tell you the results."

F « Salut ! Nous faisons un sondage et j'ai besoin de votre numéro de téléphone. Si vous me le donnez, je vous rappelle et je vous donne les résultats. »

D „ Hallo, ich mache eine Meinungsumfrage und brauche Ihre Telefonnummer. Wenn Sie sie mir geben, rufe ich Sie an und sage Ihnen das Ergebnis. "

I "Ciao, stiamo facendo un sondaggio e ho bisogno del tuo numero di telefono. Se me lo dai, ti chiamo e ti farò sapere i risultati."

E "Hola, estamos haciendo un estudio y necesito tu número de teléfono. Si me lo das, te llamaré y te daré los resultados."

P "Olá, estamos a fazer uma pesquisa e precisamos do seu número de telefone. Se mo der, telefonarei para si a comunicar os resultados."

S "Hej, vi håller på med en enkät och jag behöver ditt telefonnummer. Om du ger mig det så ringer jag dig och meddelar resultatet."

The Bar...

GB [Look at the label in his shirt and say] "I wanted to see if you were really made in Hong Kong."

F [Regarder l'étiquette sur sa chemise et dire] « Je voulais voir si vous étiez vraiment fabriqué à Hong Kong. »

D (Sehen Sie sich das Etikett in seinem Hemd an und sagen:) „Ich wollte nur mal sehen, ob Sie wirklich in Hong Kong hergestellt wurden."

I [Leggi l'etichetta sulla sua camicia e digli] "Volevo solamente vedere se sei veramente Made in Hong Kong."

E [Mira la etiqueta de su camisa y di:] "Quería saber si realmente estabas hecho en Hong Kong."

P [Olha para a etiqueta na camisola dele e diz:] "Queria ver se foste realmente feito em Hong Kong."

S [Titta på etiketten i hans skjorta och säg:] "Jag ville se om du verkligen gjordes i Hong Kong."

The Bar...

GB My drink is getting lonely. Would you like to join me with yours?"

F « Mon verre s'ennuie tout seul. Est-ce que votre verre veut bien le rejoindre? »

D „ Mein Getränk fühlt sich einsam. Würden Sie meinem Glas mit dem Ihrem Gesellschaft leisten? "

I "Il mio bicchiere si sente solo. Vorresti tenergli compagnia con il tuo?"

E "Mi bebida se siente sola. ¿Te gustaría acompañarme con la tuya?"

P "A minha bebida está a ficar solitária. Quer juntar-se a mim com a sua?"

S "Min drink börjar känna sig ensam. Vill du slå dig ner med din?"

The Bar...

GB "Do you know what winks and makes love like a panther?" [Then wink]

F « Qu'est ce qui fait des clins d'œil et fait l'amour comme une panthère ? » [Ensuite faire un·clin d'œil]

D „Wissen Sie, was blinzelt und wie ein Panther im Bett ist ? (Dann blinzeln)"

I "Sai chi fa l'occhiolino e l'amore come una pantera?" [Poi fagli l'occhiolino]

E "¿Sabes qué guiña y hace el amor como una pantera?" [Luego guiña el ojo]

P "Sabe o que pisca os olhos e faz amor como uma pantera?" [Depois pisca os olhos]

S "Vet du vad som blinkar och älskar som en panter?" [Blinka sedan]

The Bar...

GB "Have you always been this cute, or did you have to work at it?"

F «Avez-vous toujours été aussi mignon ou est ce que vous avez fait des efforts ? »

D „Waren Sie schon immer so niedlich oder mussten Sie daran arbeiten ? "

I "Sei sempre così carino, o ci ha lavorato su parecchio per diventarlo?"

E "¿Siempre has sido tan guapo o has tenido que trabajarlo?"

P "Você foi sempre assim giro, ou teve que trabalhar para isso?"

S "Har du alltid varit så här söt eller var du tvungen att jobba på det?"

GB "I think you're the light at the end of my tunnel."

F « Je crois que vous êtes la lumière au bout de mon tunnel. »

D „Ich glaube, Sie sind das Licht am Ende des Tunnels ."

I "Credo che tu sia la luce all'uscita del mio tunnel."

E "Eres la luz al final de mi túnel."

P "Penso que és a luz no fundo do meu túnel."

S "Jag tror att du är ljuset i slutet på min tunnel."

The Bar...

GB "I'm doing a survey. After sex, do you run off or do you start snoring?"

F «Je fais un sondage. Après l'amour, vous fuyez ou vous ronfler ? »

D „ Ich mache eine Meinungsumfrage. Nach dem Sie Sex gehabt haben, laufen Sie weg oder schnarchen Sie ? "

I "Sto facendo un sondaggio. Dopo avere fatto l'amore, te ne vai o cominci a russare?"

E "Estoy haciendo un estudio. Después de hacer el amor ¿te largas o te pones a roncar?"

P "Estou a fazer uma pesquisa. Depois do sexo, vai-se embora ou começ a ressonar?"

S "Jag håller på med en enkät. Springer du din väg eller börjar du snarka efter att du har älskat?"

GB "My name is [your name], but you can call me anything at all, so long as you call me."

F « Je m'appelle [votre nom], mais vous pouvez m'appelez comme vous voulez, tant que vous m'appeler. »

D „ Mein Name ist (Ihr Name), aber Sie können mich nennen wie Sie wollen, solange Sie sich mal melden. "

I "Mi chiamo [il tuo nome], ma tu puoi chiamarmi come vuoi, l'importante è che mi chiami."

E "Me llamo [tu nombre], pero puedes llamarme de cualquier manera, con tal de que me llames."

P "O meu nome é [o nome], mas podes chamar-me qualquer coisa, desde que me chames."

S "Jag heter [ditt namn], men du kan kalla mig älskling när du ringer."

The Bar...

GB "Excuse me, I'm a little short on cash. Would you mind if we shared a cab home together?"

F « Excusez-moi, je n'ai plus de liquide, ça vous embête si nous partageons un taxi pour rentrer? »

D „Entschuldigung, ich habe etwas wenig Geld bei mir. Hätten Sie etwas dagegen, wenn wir uns ein Taxi nach Hause teilen?"

I "Mi scusi, ma mi restano pochi spiccioli. Le dispiacerebbe dividere il taxi fino a casa con me?"

E "Perdona, no llevo mucho dinero. ¿Te importaría compartir juntos un taxi a casa?"

P "Desculpe, estou com pouco dinheiro. Importa-se se formos no mesmo táxi para casa?"

S "Ursäkta mig, jag har lite dåligt med kontanter. Skulle du ha något emot att dela en taxi hem med mig?"

The Bar...

GB "Hi, I'd like to know what sort of man would go out dressed like that?"

F « Salut, mais quel est le type qui sortirait habillé comme ça? »

D „ Hallo, ich möchte gern mal wissen, welche Sorte Mann so angezogen aus dem Haus geht. "

I "Ciao, mi piacerebbe conoscere il tipo di uomo che va in giro vestito in questo modo."

E "Hola. Me gustaría saber qué clase de hombre saldría a la calle vestido de esta manera."

P "Olá, gostaria de saber que tipo de homem sairía à rua vestido dessa maneira."

S "Hej, jag skulle vilja veta vad för sorts man som går ut klädd så där?"

The Bar...

GB "I'm becoming a nun tomorrow. How about one last sin?"

F « Je deviens nonne demain. Ça vous dit un dernier pêché? »

D „Ich gehe morgen ins Kloster. Möchten Sie meine letzte Sünde sein?"

I "Domani mi faccio suora. Che cosa ne pensi se commetto l'ultimo peccato con te?"

E "Mañana me hago monja. ¿Qué tal un último pecado?"

P "A partir de amanhã vou para madre. Que tal um último pecado?"

S "Jag blir nunna i morgon. Vad sägs om en sista synd?"

The Bar...

GB
"I'm sorry, were you talking to me? Well please start, then!"

F
« Excusez-moi vous me disiez quelque chose ? Eh bien allez-y ! »

D
„Entschuldigung. Sprechen Sie mit mir ? Ah, dann fangen Sie mal ruhig an. "

I
"Mi scusi, sta parlando con me? No. Bene, allora comincia!"

E
"Perdona ¿hablabas conmigo? Bueno pues entonces, empieza ya por favor."

P
"Desculpe, estava a falar comigo? Bem, então pode começar."

S
"Ursäkta, talade du till mig? Nähä, men sätt i gång då!"

The Bar...

GB "Would you mind taking your clothes off? I would like to compare the image in my mind with the real thing."

F « Ça vous dérangerait de vous déshabiller ? J'aimerais comparer l'image que j'ai en tête avec la réalité. »

D „Würden Sie sich bitte ausziehen ? Ich möchte meine Vorstellung gerne mit der Wirklichkeit vergleichen. "

I "Ti dispiace spogliarti? Vorrei vedere se l'immagine che ho di te nella mia mente è uguale alla realtà."

E "¿Te importaría sacarte la ropa? Me gustaría comparar la imagen en mi imaginación con la real."

P "Não se importa de se despir? Gostaria de comparar a imagem na minha cabeça com a coisa real."

S "Skulle du ha något emot att ta av dig kläderna? Jag vill jämföra bilden i min fantasi med den äkta varan?"

The Bar...

GB "You must be a great thief because you stole my heart from across the room."

F « Vous devez être un voleur hors pair parce que vous avez volé mon cœur qui était à l'autre bout de la pièce. »

D „ Sie müssen ein Meisterdieb sein, so wie Sie mein Herz aus der Ferne gestohlen haben. "

I "Devi essere un ladro molto esperto perchè sei riuscito a rubare il mio cuore."

E "Debes ser un gran ladrón porque me has robado el corazón desde la otra punta de la sala."

P "Você deve ser um grande ladrão porque roubou o meu coração do outro lado da sala."

S "Du måste vara en mycket duktig tjuv eftersom du lyckades stjäla mitt hjärta från andra sidan rummet."

The Bar...

GB "Can you believe that just a few hours ago we'd never even been to bed together?"

F « Est-ce que tu te rends compte qu'il y a une demi heure nous n'avions jamais été au lit ensemble ? »

D „Kaum zu glauben, dass wir noch vor wenigen Stunden niemals miteinander im Bett waren. "

I "Ci credi che fino a poche ore fa non eravamo mai stati a letto insieme?"

E "¿Puedes creerte que hace sólo unas horas ni siquiera nos habíamos acostado nunca juntos?"

P "Você acredita que há apenas algumas horas nunca tínhamos ido para a cama juntos?"

S "Kan du tänka dig att för bara ett par timmar sedan hade vi inte ens gått till sängs med varandra?"

The Bar...

GB "I'm told that virginity can be highly over-rated!"

F « On dit que la virginité est très surfaite de nos jours ! »

D „ Ich habe irgendwo gehört, dass Jungfräulichkeit überbewertet wird. "

I "Mi è stato detto che la verginità può essere sopravvalutata!"

E "Me han dicho que la virginidad puede estar altamente sobrevalorada."

P "Disseram-me que a virgindade pode ser altamente hiper-valorizada."

S "Jag har hört att oskulden är högt överskattad!"

The Bar...

GB "Nice to meet you, I'm [your name] and you are gorgeous!"

F « Heureuse de vous rencontrer. Je m'appelle [votre nom] et vous vous appelez superbe ! »

D „Schön, Sie kennenzulernen. Ich heiße (Ihr Name) und Sie sehen umwerfend aus."

I "Piacere di conoscerti, mi chiamo [il tuo nome] e sei bellissimo!"

E "Encantada de conocerte, soy [tu nombre] y estás para comerte."

P "Prazer em conhecê-lo, eu sou a [nome] e tu és jeitoso."

S "Trevligt att träffas, mitt namn är [ditt namn] och ditt måste vara underbar!"

The Bar...

GB "What do you do when you're not standing around looking hunkish?"

F « Eh beau mec ! Qu'est-ce que vous faites dans la vie quand vous ne restez pas planté là? »

D „Was machen Sie denn, wenn Sie nicht einfach rumstehen und gut aussehen ? "

I "Che cosa fai a parte essere un così bel pezzo di ragazzo?"

E "¿A qué te dedicas cuando no andas por ahí con este aspecto de tío bueno?"

P "O que é que fazes quando não estás parado a olhar com essas peneiras todas?"

S "Vad sysslar du med när du inte hänger i baren och ser djurisk ut?"

The Bar...

GB "You look confused. Drink I can you a buy?"

F « Tu as l'air embrouillé. Verre moi offrir toi ? »

D „ Sie sehen verwirrt aus, kann ich Ihnen einen ausgeben ? "

I "Mi sembri confuso. Offrirti bere posso da?"

E "Pareces confundido. ¿Copa una puedo a te invitar?"

P "Pareces-me confuso. Bebida eu posso uma oferecer?"

S "Du ser förvirrad ut. Drink jag får en bjuda på?"

The Bar...

GB "Do you believe in one-night stands?"

F « Vous y croyez aux histoires d'une nuit ? »

D „Halten Sie One-Night Stands für eine gute Idee ? "

I "Credi in una notte d'amore?"

E "¿Crees en rollos de una noche?"

P "Acreditas em directas, ficar acordado toda a noite?"

S "Tror du på one-night stands?"

The Bar...

GB "I want to have your babies, but there's not much time – quick, let's get started!"

F « Je veux avoir vos bébés mais le temps presse, allez on y va ! »

D „Ich will Ihre Babys, aber wir haben nicht viel Zeit – schnell, lassen Sie uns anfangen."

I "Voglio avere i tuoi bambini, ma non abbiamo molto tempo – sbrigati, diamoci da fare!"

E "Quiero tener tus hijos, pero no tenemos mucho tiempo, ¡rápido, empecemos ya!"

P "Quero ter os teus filhos, mas não tempos muito tempo rápido, vamos começar."

S "Jag vill föda dina barn, men vi har inte mycket tid kvar – det är bäst att vi skyndar oss!"

The Disco...

The Disco...

GB "What would you do if I kissed you right now?"

F « Qu'est ce que tu fais si je t'embrasse maintenant ? »

D „Was würden Sie tun, wenn ich Sie jetzt küsse ? "

I "Che cosa faresti se ti baciassi?"

E "¿Qué harías si te besara ahora mismo?"

P "O que faria se o beijasse neste preciso momento?"

S "Vad skulle du göra om jag kysste dig nu?"

The Disco...

GB "If it's sex you're looking for, just take me home now. No need to spend any more time here."

F « Si tu es là pour le sexe, emmène-moi à la maison maintenant. Inutile de perdre du temps. »

D „Fall es Sex ist, wonach Sie suchen, nehmen Sie mich einfach mit nach Hause. Es ist nicht nötig, hier noch mehr Zeit zu verschwenden. "

I "Se vuoi del sesso, portami a casa tua adesso. Non sprechiamo altro tempo qui dentro."

E "Si lo que buscas es sexo, ya puedes llevarme a casa. No hay necesidad de pasar más tiempo aquí."

P Se é de sexo que está à procura, leve-me já para casa. Não precisamos de passar mais tempo aqui."

S "Om det är sex du är ute efter kan du ta med mig hem nu. Finns ingen anledning att ödsla mer tid här, eller hur?"

The Disco...

GB "I think I could fall madly in bed with you."

F «Je crois que je pourrais tomber follement dans ton lit.»

D „Ich glaube ich könnte wie verrückt mit Ihnen ins Bett fallen."

I "Penso che potrei venire perdutamente a letto con te."

E "Creo que podría enamorarme locamente de tu cama."

P "Eu penso que posso cair loucamente na cama consigo."

S "Vi är som magneter. Din nord mot min syd."

The Disco...

GB "I can tell that you're a terrific lover, and it scares me."

F « Tu dois être un amant terrible et ça me terrifie. »

D „ Ich habe so eine Ahnung, dass Sie ein großartiger Liebhaber sind und das macht mir Angst. "

I "Posso capire che sei un amante formidabile e questo mi intimorisce."

E "Se nota que eres un amante fabuloso, y eso me asusta."

P "Posso dizer que és um amante terrível, e isto assusta-me."

S "Jag kan se att du är en underbar älskare och det skrämmer mig."

The Disco...

GB "Hi, I have been watching you dance over there for a while now, and to be honest, you're dreadful. Buy me a drink and we can talk about it."

F « Salut ! Je te regarde danser depuis tout à l'heure et franchement, c'est la catastrophe. Offre moi un verre et on en parlera. »

D „ Hallo, ich habe Ihnen eine Weile beim Tanzen zugesehen, und um ganz ehrlich zu sein, Sie tanzen schrecklich schlecht. Ich gebe Ihnen einen aus und wir können darüber reden. "

I "Ciao, ti sto osservando da un po', e per dirti la verità, il tuo modo di ballare fa proprio pena. Offrimi da bere e possiamo discuterne."

E "Hola. Llevo un rato mirando como bailas, y si he de sert sincera, eres malísimo. Déjame invitarte a una copa y hablamos de ello."

P "Olá, tenho estado a apreciar a sua maneira de dançar há algum tempo e, para ser honesta, você é espantoso. Ofereça-me uma bebida e poderemos falar sobre isso."

S "Hej, jag har iakttagit dig dansa ett tag nu, och ärligt talat så dansar du uselt. Bjud mig på en drink så kan vi tala om det."

The Disco...

GB "So, what does it take for a girl like me to get your phone-number?"

F « Qu'est-ce qu'une pauvre fille comme moi doit faire pour avoir ton numéro de téléphone ? »

D „So, was muss ein Mädchen wie ich tun, um Ihre Telefonnummer zu bekommen ? "

I "E allora che cosa deve fare una ragazza come me per avere il tuo numero di telefono?"

E "¿Qué tiene que hacer una chica como yo para conseguir tu número de teléfono?"

P "O que é que uma raparigo como eu tem que fazer para conseguir o teu número de telefone?"

S "Vad krävs det av en tjej som mig för att få ditt telefonnummer?"

The Disco...

GB Can I borrow some change? I want to call your mother and thank her."

F « Est-ce que je peux t'emprunter de la monnaie ? Je voudrais appeler ta mère pour la remercier. »

D „ Können Sie mir etwas Kleingeld leihen ? Ich möchte mich bei Ihrer Mutter bedanken. "

I "Puoi prestarmi della moneta? Voglio chiamare tua madre per ringraziarla."

E "¿Tienes cambio? Quiero llamar a tu madre y darle las gracias."

P "Emprestas-me alguns trocos? Quero telefonar à tua mãe a agradecer."

S "Kan jag låna lite småmynt? Jag vill ringa din mamma och tacka henne."

The Disco...

GB [As he leaves] "Hey, aren't you forgetting something? Me!"

F [Alors qu'il part] « Hé, tu n'oublie pas quelque chose là ? Moi ! »

D (Wenn er geht) „Hallo, vergessen Sie da nicht etwas? Mich ? "

I [Mentre lui se ne sta andando] "Ehi, non ti stai dimenticando qualcosa? Me!"

E [Cuando se marcha] "¡Oye! ¿No olvidas algo? ¡A mí!"

P [Quando ele sai] "Ei, não se está a esquecer de nada? Eu."

S [När han går:] "Du, glömmer du inte någonting nu? Mig?"

The Disco...

GB "I'm not above begging!"

F « Ça ne me gênerait pas de me mettre à genoux ! »

D „Ich bin mir nicht zu schade zum Betteln."

I "Non mi vergogno affatto di implorare."

E "Si quieres te hago un favor."

P "Até sou capaz de implorar."

S "Jag kan till och med tigga om det skulle få dig att säga ja."

The Disco...

GB "Aren't you my blind date for tonight?"

F « C'est toi mon inconnu de la soirée ? »

D „Sind Sie nicht mein Blind Date für heute Abend ? "

I "Non saresti per caso il mio amante segreto per questa notte?"

E "¿No eres tú mi cita a ciegas de esta noche?"

P "Não é você o meu par esta noite?"

S "Är inte du min blind date i kväll?"

The Disco...

GB "Screw me if I'm wrong, but don't you want to kiss me?"

F « Baise-moi si je me trompe mais tu n'aurais pas envie de m'embrasser par hasard ? »

D „Ich kann mich ja irren, aber wollen Sie mich nicht küssen ? "

I "Che sia fottuta se non ho ragione, ma non vorresti baciarmi?"

E "Que me jodan si me equivoco, pero ¿no quieres besarme?"

P "Pape-me se estiver errada, mas você quer beijar-me, não quer?"

S "Jag kan ha fel men du vill väl kyssa mig?"

The Disco...

GB "I'm single!"

F «Je suis célibataire!»

D „Ich bin Single."

I "Non ho legami!"

E "Soltera y sin compromiso."

P "Sou solteira!"

S "Jag är singel!"

The Disco...

GB "You have one of the best bodies I've seen so far."

F « C'est l'un des plus beaux corps que j'aie vue jusqu'à présent. »

D „ Sie haben den besten Körper, den ich bis heute gesehen habe. "

I "Hai uno dei corpi più belli che abbia mai visto."

E "Tienes uno de los mejores cuerpos que he visto en mi vida."

P Você tem um dos corpos mais bonitos que já vi até hoje."

S "Du har en av de vackraste kroppar jag har sett hittills."

The Disco...

GB "Your hair and my pillow are perfectly colour co-ordinated."

F « Mon oreiller et tes cheveux ont des couleurs tout à fait assorties. »

D „ Ihr Haar und mein Kopfkissen passen farblich perfekt zueinander. "

I "Il colore dei tuoi capelli è in sintonia perfetta con il colore del mio cuscino."

E "Tu pelo quedaría estupendamente en mi almohada."

P "O teu cabelo e a minha almofada condizem perfeitamente."

S "Din hårfärg och min kudde matchar varandra perfekt."

The Disco...

GB "Fancy coming back to my place and doing the things I'll tell everyone we did anyway?"

F « Ça te dit de rentrer chez moi et de faire des choses que je raconterai de toutes façons à tout le monde ? »

D „ Haben Sie Lust mit zu mir zu kommen und alles das zu tun, was ich allen anderen morgen sowieso erzählen werde ? "

I "Vorresti passare la notte da me e fare tutte quelle cose che comunque racconterei a tutti che abbiamo fatto?"

E "¿Te apetece venir a mi casa a hacer lo que de todas maneras diré que hemos hecho?"

P "Gostarias de ir a minha casa e fazer as coisas que de qualquer forma direi às pessoas que fizemos?"

S "Har du lust att följa med hem och göra alla de saker som jag kommer att berätta för alla att vi gjorde ändå?"

The Disco...

GB "I hope you know mouth-to-mouth resuscitation, because you're taking my breath away."

F « J'espère que tu sais faire le bouche à bouche parce que tu me coupes le souffle. »

D „ Ich hoffe Sie kennen sich mit Mund-zu Mund Beatmung aus, mir bleibt nämlich grade die Luft weg. "

I "Spero che sai fare la respirazione bocca a bocca perchè mi stai facendo mancare il respiro."

E "Espero que sepas de reanimación boca a boca porque me estás dejando sin respiración."

P "Espero que saiba fazer respiração boca-a-boca, porque você está a tirar-me o fôlego."

S "Jag hoppas du kan mun-mot-mun-metoden för du får mig att tappa andan."

The Disco...

GB "I've got a condom with your name on it."

F «J'ai un préservatif avec ton nom écrit dessus.»

D „Ich habe ein Kondom mit Ihrem Namen drauf."

I "Ho un preservativo con sopra il tuo nome."

E "Tengo un condón que lleva tu nombre."

P "Tenho uma camisinha com o teu nome."

S "Jag har en kondom som bär ditt namn."

GB "My name's [your name], but you can call me lover."

F « Je m'appelle [votre nom] mais tu peux m'appeler chérie. »

D „Mein Name ist (Ihr Name) aber Sie können mich Liebling nennen."

I "Mi chiamo [il tuo nome], ma tu mi puoi chiamare amante."

E "Me llamo [tu nombre], pero puedes llamarme amante."

P "O meu nome é [o nome], mas podes chamar-me amante."

S "Jag heter [ditt namn], men du kan kalla mig älskling."

The Disco...

GB "Stand still. 1 want to pick you up."

F « Bouge pas, je viens t'emballer »

D „ Stehen Sie bitte still – ich möchte Sie abschleppen. "

I "Stai fermo. Voglio rimorchiarti."

E "No te muevas. Quiero ligar contigo."

P "Fica quieto. Quero debicar-te."

S "Stå stilla. Jag vill stöta på dig."

The Disco...

GB "You look like the type of guy who has heard every line in the book, so what's one more?"

F « Tu as l'air du type qui connaît par cœur le petit guide du parfait dragueur . Alors, c'est quoi la suite ? »

D „ Sie sehen aus wie jemand, der schon alle Abschleppnummern gehört hat,- was macht eine mehr schon aus ? "

I "Mi sembri quel tipo di giovanotto che ne ha provate di tutte, quindi una in più non farà tanta differenza."

E "Pareces el tipo de chico que ya ha oído todo tipo de cumplidos, ¿qué más da otro?"

P "Você parece o tipo de homem que já ouviu todo o tipo de propostas, por isso mais uma que diferença faz?"

S "Du ser ut som den sortens tjej som har hört alla raggningsrepliker så vad spelar en till för roll?"

The Office...

GB "Can l flirt with you?"

F « Est-ce que je peux flirter avec vous? »

D „ Kann Ich mit Ihnen flirten ? "

I "Posso farti la corte?"

E "¿Puedo ligar contigo?"

P "Queres namoriscar comigo?"

S "Får jag flirta med dig?"

The Office...

GB "I miss my teddy bear. Would you sleep with me?"

F «J'ai besoin d'un nounours. Vous voulez bien dormir avec moi ? »

D „Mein Teddy fehlt mir, können Sie mit mir zu Bett kommen ? "

I "Mi manca il mio orsacchiotto. Vuoi dormire con me?"

E "Hecho de menos a mi osito. ¿Te importaría dormir conmigo?"

P "Perdi o meu urso de peluche. Queres dormir comigo?"

S "Jag saknar min nallebjörn. Vill du sova med mig?"

The Office...

GB "You look better than my husband's expense account."

F « Vous avez meilleure mine que le compte en banque de mon mari. »

D „ Sie sehen besser aus, als das Spesenkonto meines Mannes. "

I "Sei più in forma del conto corrente di mio marito."

E "Tienes mejor aspecto que la cuenta de gastos de mi marido."

P "Pareces-me melhor do que a conta de despesas do meu marido."

S "Du ser bättre ut än min mans representationskonto."

The Office...

GB "Do you believe in love at first sight, or do I have to walk by again?"

F «Vous croyez au coup de foudre ou je dois recommencer mon entrée ? »

D „Glauben Sie an Liebe auf den ersten Blick oder soll ich noch einmal vorbeikommen ? "

I "Credi nell'amore a prima vista o devo rientrare un'altra volta?"

E "¿Crees en el amor a primera vista o tengo que volver a pasar otra vez?"

P "Acreditas no amor à primeira vista, ou tenho que passar outra vez?"

S "Tror du på kärlek vid första ögonkastet eller skall jag behöva gå förbi en gång till?"

The Office...

GB   "Are you married, or happy?"

F   « Etes-vous heureux ou...marié ? »

D   „ Sie sind verheiratet oder glücklich ? "

I   "Sei sposato o sei felice?"

E   "¿Estás casado o eres feliz?"

P   "Você é feliz, ou casado?"

S   "Är du gift eller lycklig?"

The Office...

GB "Did you know that I wrote the Kama Sutra?"

F « Savez-vous que j'ai écrit le Kama Sutra? »

D „Wußten Sie schon, dass ich das Kama Sutra geschrieben habe? "

I "Lo sapevi che ho scritto io il Kama Sutra?"

E "¿Sabías que yo escribí el Kama Sutra?"

P "Sabia que eu escrevi o Kama Sutra?"

S "Visste du att det var jag som skrev Kama Sutra?"

GB "I'm no good at opening lines, so why don't we pretend we know each other?"

F «Je ne suis pas très doué pour la drague. On fait comme si on se connaissait ? »

D „Ich bin nicht besonders gut beim Kennenlernen, können wir vielleicht so tun, als ob wir uns schon kennen ? "

I "Non sono tanto brava a rompere il ghiaccio, perchè allora non facciamo finta che ci conosciamo di già?"

E "No se me dan nada bien las presentaciones. ¿Por qué no fingimos que ya nos conocemos?"

P "Não sou boa em apresentações, por isso porque não fingimos que nos conhecemos ?"

S "Jag är inget bra på kallprat så vi kan väl låtsas att vi känner varandra?"

The Office...

GB "Add some enjoyment to someone's day. Mine for instance."

F « Mettez un peu de joie à la journée de quelqu'un. La mienne par exemple. »

D „ Machen Sie jemanden glücklich, mich zum Beispiel. "

I "Dai, rendi più piacevole la giornata a qualcuno. A me pe esempio."

E "Aporta algo de felicidad al día de alguna persona. Al mí por ejemplo."

P "Acrescenta alguma alegria ao dia de alguém. Ao meu, por exemplo."

S "Gör någons dag mer njutbar. Min till exempel."

The Office...

GB "Let's do breakfast tomorrow – should I call you or nudge you?"

F « On prend le petit déjeuner ensemble, demain. Je vous appelle ou je dois vous donner un coup de coude ? »

D „ Lassen Sie uns Morgen zusammen frühstücken – soll ich Sie anrufen oder Ihnen auf die Schulter tippen ? "

I "Facciamo colazione assieme domani – per svegliarti devo chimarti o darti una gomitata?"

E "Desayunemos juntos mañana, ¿te llamo o te despierto de un codazo"

P "Vamos tomar o pequeno almoço juntos amanhã. Chamo-te com um telefonema ou com uma cotovelada?"

S "Vi kan väl äta frukost i morgon – skall jag ringa och väcka dig eller bara knuffa till dig?"

The Office...

GB "My friends call me Orange. Want to squeeze me?"

F « Mes amis m'appelle orange. Vous voulez la presser ? »

D „Meine Freunde nennen mich Apfelsine – Wollen Sie mich drücken ? "

I "I miei amici mi chiamano Arancia. Vuoi spremermi?"

E "Mis amigos me llaman Naranja. ¿Quieres exprimirme?"

P "Os meus amigos chamam-me Laranja. Queres espremer-me?"

S "Mina vänner kallar mig koalan. Jag är så kramgo!"

The Office...

GB "My mother told me to stay away from men like you. Why not prove her wrong?"

F « Ma mère m'a dit de ne pas parler avec des hommes comme vous. On lui prouve qu'elle a tort ? »

D „Meine Mutter hat mich vor Männern wie Ihnen gewarnt. Wollen Sie ihr nicht beweisen, dass sie unrecht hatte ? "

I "Mia madre mi ha sempre detto di stare alla larga dagli uomini come te. Perchè non proviamo a vedere se ha torto?"

E "Mi madre me dijo que me alejara de hombres como tú. ¿Por qué no demostramos que se equivoca?"

P "A minha mãe disse-me para ficar longe de homens como tu. Porque não provamos que ela está errada?"

S "Min mor sa till mig att hålla mig borta från män som du. Bevisa att hon hade fel!"

The Office...

GB "Nice suit. Can I talk you out of it?"

F «Joli costume, je peux le mettre à nu?»

D „Schöner Anzug. Kann ich Sie dazu bringen, ihn auszuziehen?"

I "Bel completo. Posso convincerti a sfilarlo per me?"

E "Bonito traje. ¿Puedo convencerte de que te lo quites?"

P "Bonito fato. Posso tirar-te de dentro dele?"

S "Snygg kostym. Men du är nog snyggare utan."

The Office...

GB "You turn my system on."

F «Vous allumez mon système .»

D „ Sie machen mein System an. "

I "Mi ecciti il mio sistema."

E "Has puesto en marcha mi sistema."

P "Você põe o meu sistema a funcionar."

S "Vill du se på min hårddisk."

The Office...

GB "Do you believe in fate?"

F «Vous croyez au destin?»

D „Glauben Sie an Fügung?"

I "Credi al destino?"

E "¿Crees en el destino?"

P "Acredita no destino?"

S "Tror du på ödet?"

The Office...

GB "You know, you're very easy on the eyes!"

F « Vous savez, on ne se lasse pas de vous regarder ! »

D „Wissen Sie, Sie sind sehr einfach anzustarren. "

I "Sai che sei proprio un piacere per gli occhi!"

E "Sabes, no cuesta nada mirarte."

P "Sabes, à primeira vista pareces ser fácil de levar!"

S "Mina trötta ögon vilar lätt på dig."

Over the top...

Over the top...

GB "I'm in the process of writing a telephone book. May I take your number?"

F « Je rédige actuellement un annuaire téléphonique. Puis-je avoir votre numéro ? »

D „ Ich schreibe gerade ein Telefonbuch. Kann ich Ihre Nummer haben ? "

I "Sto scrivendo una guida telefonica. Posso avere il tuo numero di telefono?"

E "Estoy escribiendo una guía telefónica. ¿Me das tu número?"

P "Estou a preparar uma lista telefónica. Posso ter o seu número?"

S "Jag håller på att skriva en telefonbok. Kan jag få ditt nummer?"

Over the top...

GB "I'm not drunk, I'm just intoxicated by you."

F «Je ne suis pas saoule. C'est juste que je suis ivre de vous. »

D „Ich bin nicht betrunken, Sie haben mich berauscht. "

I "Non sono ubriaca, sei tu che mi hai inebriata."

E "No es que esté borracha, es que me embriagas."

P "Não estou bêbada, estou apenas intoxicada por si."

S "Jag är inte full, det är du som berusar mig."

Over the top...

GB "Oh, those are shoulder blades, I thought they might be wings."

F « Ah , ce sont vos omoplates ! Je croyais que c'était des ailes . »

D „Ah, das sind Schulterblätter, und ich dachte das seien Flügel. "

I "Oh, sono solo le tue spalle, pensavo fossero ali."

E "¡Ah! Son omoplatos, pensaba que eran alas."

P "Oh, são chumaços para os ombros, pensei que fossem asas."

S "Jaså, är det skulderblad. Jag som trodde det var vingar."

Over the top...

GB "Why did the girl cross the dance floor? Because she fell in love with the guy at the bar."

F « Pourquoi cette fille a-t-elle traversé la piste de danse ? Parce qu'elle est tombée amoureuse du type au bar. »

D „Warum dieses Mädchen über die Tanzfläche hierher gekommen ist ? Sie hat sich in den Mann an der Theke verliebt . "

I "Perchè la ragazza ha attraversato tutta la sala da ballo? Perchè si è follemente innamorata del ragazzo seduto al bar."

E "¿Por qué cruzó la chica la pista de baile? Porque se enamoró del tipo del bar. "

P "Por que razão a rapariga atravessou a pista de dança? Porque se apaixonou pelo rapaz que está no bar."

S "Varför gick tjejen över dansgolvet? Hon blev kär i killen i baren."

Over the top...

GB "Are you religious? Good, I'm the answer to your prayers."

F «Vous êtes croyant? Bon, je suis la réponse à vos prières»

D „Sind Sie gläubig? Gut, ich bin die Antwort auf Ihre Gebete. "

I "Sei religioso? Ottimo, perchè io sono la risposta alle tue preghiere."

E "¿Eres religioso? Qué bien, yo soy la respuesta a tus plegarias."

P "Es religioso? Óptimo, tenho a resposta para as tuas orações."

S "Är du religiös? Bra. Jag är svaret på dina böner."

Over the top...

GB "Hello, I'm a thief, and I'm here to steal your heart."

F « Bonjour, je suis un voleur et je suis venu voler votre cœur. »

D „ Hallo, ich bin ein Dieb und bin hier um Ihr Herz zu stehlen. "

I "Ciao, sono una ladra e sono qui per rubare il tuo cuore."

E "Hola, soy una ladrona y estoy aquí para robarte el corazón."

P "Olá, sou um ladrão, e estou aqui para roubar o teu coração."

S "Hej, jag är tjuv och jag är här för att stjäla ditt hjärta."

Over the top...

GB "If your parents had never met, I'd be a very unhappy woman."

F « Si vos parents ne s'étaient pas rencontrés, j'aurais été très malheureuse. »

D „Wenn Ihre Eltern sich nie kennengelernt hätten, wäre ich jetzt sehr unglücklich. "

I "Se i tuoi genitori non si fossero mai incontrati, a quest'ora sarei stata una donna veramente infelice."

E "Si tus padres no se hubieran conocido, ahora mismo yo sería una mujer muy desgraciada."

P "Se os teu pais não se tivessem conhecido, eu era uma mulher muito infeliz."

S "Om dina föräldrar aldrig hade träffats skulle jag vara en mycket olycklig kvinna."

Over the top...

GB "Is it hot in here or is it just you?"

F « Il faut chaud ici ou c'est toi ? »

D „ Ist es heiß hier, oder sind Sie das ? "

I "Fa caldo qui dentro o sei tu che mi stai facendo alzare la temperatura?"

E "Hace calor aquí ¿no? ¿O eres tú?"

P "Aqui está realmente quente, ou é apenas você?"

S "Är det varmt härinne eller är det du som är het?"

Over the top...

GB "I didn't know angels flew so low."

F « Je ne savais pas que les anges pouvaient descendre si près de nous. »

D „ Ich wußte gar nicht, das Engel so tief fliegen. "

I "Non sapevo che gli angeli potessero volare così in basso."

E "No sabía que los ángeles volaran tan bajo."

P "Não sabia que os anjos voavam tão baixo."

S "Jag visste inte att änglar flög så lågt."

Over the top...

GB "I was sitting here holding a cigarette and I realised I'd rather be holding you."

F « J'étais assise avec ma cigarette à la main et je me suis rendu compte que je préférerais t'avoir toi dans la main. »

D „Ich habe hier einfach gesessen und meine Zigarette festgehalten, und dann habe ich gemerkt, dass ich viel lieber Sie festhalten würde."

I "Ero là seduta con una sigaretta tra le labbra, quando mi sono resa conto che preferirei avere te fra le mie labbra."

E "Estaba sentada aquí tomándome algo y me he dado cuenta de que preferiría tenerte a ti en lugar de la copa."

P "Estou aqui sentada a segurar um cigarro e dei conta que devia era estar a segurar noutra coisa, em ti."

S "Jag satt här och höll i en cigarett när jag insåg att jag hellre håller i dig."

Over the top...

GB "Somebody call the police, because it's got to be illegal to look that good."

F « Ce doit être illégal d'être aussi beau. Mais que fait la police ? »

D „Kann bitte jemand die Polizei rufen, es ist kriminell so gut auszusehen, "

I "Qualcuno chiami la polizia; è sicuramente un crimine essere così belli."

E "Que alguien llame a la policía. Tendría que ser ilegal ser tan guapo."

P "Alguém chame a polícia, porque tem que ser ilegal ter um ar tão bem parecido."

S "Ring polisen, det måste vara olagligt att vara så snygg."

Over the top...

GB "Were you in the Boy Scouts? You have certainly tied my heart in a knot."

F «Vous étiez chez les scouts, non? Vous avez fait un nœud avec mon cœur!»

D „Waren Sie bei den Pfadfindern? Sie haben einen ganz tollen Knoten in mein Herz gemacht."

I "Eri nei Boy Scouts? Perchè sei riuscito ad orientarti perfettamente nel mio cuore."

E "¿Fuiste boy scout de pequeño? Porque me has liado el corazón en un nudo."

P "Estiveste nos Escoteiros? Deste de certeza, um nó no meu coração."

S "Var du med i scouterna? Du har definitivt slagit knut på mitt hjärta."

Over the top...

GB "You must be a Greek God, and I'm betting you're in charge of cute."

F «Tu dois être un dieu grec et je parie que tu t'appelle Apollon»

D „Sie müssen ein griechischer Gott sein – ganz bestimmt zuständig für gutes Aussehen."

I "Devi essere un dio greco e scommetto che sei il dio della bellezza."

E "Debes ser un dios griego y apuesto a que eres el de la belleza."

P "Você deve ser um Deus Grego, e aposto que está encarregada da Beleza."

S "Du måste vara den grekiska gud som representerar kärleken."

Over the top...

GB "You remind me of a compass because I'd be lost without you."

F «Vous me faites pensez à une boussole parce que je serai perdue sans vous»

D „Sie erinnern mich an meinen Kompaß, ohne den fühle ich auch immer ganz aus der Bahn geworfen."

I "Mi ricordi tanto una bussola perchè sarei persa senza di te."

E "Me recuerdas a una brújula, estaría perdida sin ti."

P "Fazes-me lembrar uma bússola, porque sem ti estaria perdida."

S "Du påminner mig om en kompass för jag skulle känna mig vilsen utan dig."

Over the top...

GB "Here's 10p so you can call home and tell them you won't be home tonight."

F «Voilà un franc pour téléphoner chez vous et dire que vous ne dormirez pas à la maison ce soir»

D „Hier sind 30 Pfennig, rufen Sie Zuhause an, und sagen Bescheid, dass Sie heute Nacht nicht kommen werden."

I "Eccoti £200 per chiamare i tuoi e dire loro che non torni a casa stanotte."

E "Toma cinco duros y llama a casa a decir que esta noche no vas."

P "Tens aqui 100 escudos para telefonares para casa e dizer que esta noite não vais."

S "Här har du två kronor så att du kan ringa hem och berätta att du inte kommer hem ikväll."

Over the top...

GB "You're so hot, I had to turn off my smoke alarm."

F « Il fait si chaud ici que j'ai dû éteindre mon détecteur de fumée »

D „ Sie sind so heiß, dass ich den Rauchmelder ausschalten mußte. "

I "Sei così bollente che ho dovuto spegnere il riscaldamento."

E "Me enciendes tanto que tendré que apagar mi detector de incendios."

P "És tão quente, que tive de desligar o alarme contra incêndios."

S "Du är så eldig att jag var tvungen att stänga av mitt rökalarm."

Over the top...

GB "If I said you had a beautiful body, would you hold it against me?"

F « Si je vous disais que vous avez un corps magnifique est-ce que vous le presseriez contre le mien ? »

D „Wenn ich Ihnen sagen würde, dass Sie einen schönen Körper haben, würden Sie das gegen mich verwenden ?"

I "Se ti dicessi che hai un corpo meraviglioso, lo useresti contro di me?"

E "Si te dijera que tienes un cuerpo maravilloso ¿lo apretujarías contra el mío?"

P "Se eu lhe disser que você tem um corpo bonito, atira-o para cima de mim?"

S "Tar du illa upp om jag säger att du har en underbar kropp?"

Over the top...

GB "Is there an airport nearby or is that just my heart taking off?

F « Il y a un aéroport dans les environs ou c'est mon cœur qui plane ? »

D „ Sind wir in der Nähe vom Flughafen oder ist das mein Herz, das abhebt ? "

I "C'è un aeroporto qui vicino o è solo il mio cuore che sta prendendo il volo?"

E "¿Hay un aeropuerto por aquí cerca o es sólo mi corazón despegando?"

P "Há um aeroporto aqui perto, ou é apenas o meu coraçã a descolar?"

S "Finns det en formel-1 bana i närheten eller är det bara mitt hjärta som rivstartar?"

Over the top...

GB "Was your father a mechanic? Then how did you get such a finely-tuned body?"

F «Votre père était mécanicien? Alors comment se fait-il que vous avez des mécaniques aussi bien roulées?»

D „War Ihr Vater ein Uhrmacher? Oder wie haben Sie sonst diesen fein abgestimmten Körper bekommen?"

I "Tuo padre faceva lo scultore? No? E come fai ad avere un corpo così perfetto?"

E "¿Era mecánico tu padre? Entonces ¿cómo conseguiste un cuerpo tan bien ajustado?"

P "O teu pai era mecânico? Então como é que conseguiste um corpo tão bem afinado?"

S "Var din pappa bilmekaniker? Hur kunde du annars få en sådan vältrimmad kropp?"

Over the top...

GB "You look like you need a one-way ticket on the roly-poly express ride of love!"

F « On dirait que tu as besoin d'un aller simple pour le grand manège de l'amour ! »

D „Sie sehen aus, als ob Sie eine Karte für das Karussell der Liebe brauchen könnten."

I "Credo che hai proprio bisogno di un biglietto di sola andata sul treno dell'amore!"

E "Tienes el aspecto de necesitar un billete de ida para un revolcón urgente en el expreso del amor."

P "Você parece mesmo que precisa de um bilhete para a rocambolesca corrida do amor!"

S "Du ser ut som om du behöver en enkel biljett till kärlekens berg-och-dalbana!"

Direct...

Direct...

GB "Please may I rest my head on your shoulder?"

F « S'il te plaît, puis-je poser ma tête sur ton épaule ? »

D „Darf ich bitte meinen Kopf auf Ihre Schultern legen ? "

I "Posso posare il capo sulla tua spalla per favore?"

E "Por favor ¿puedo apoyar la cabeza en tu hombro?"

P "Por favor, posso descansar a minha cabeça no seu ombro?"

S "Får jag luta huvudet mot din axel?"

GB "You look like someone who needs to be kissed all over by a highly-skilled amateur."

F « Tu as l'air de quelqu'un dont le corps réclame les baisers d'un amateur qualifié. »

D „ Sie sehen aus, als ob von oben bis unten von einem durchtrainierten Amateur geküßt werden sollten. "

I "Mi sembri quel tipo di uomo che ha bisogno di essere baciato su tutto il corpo e da una dilettante molto esperta."

E "Tienes aspecto de necesitar que te bese por todas partes una aficionada altamente capacitada."

P "Você parece-se com alguém que precisa de ser todo beijado por uma especialista altamente qualificada."

S "Du ser ut som någon som behöver bli kysst hela natten av en skicklig amatör."

Direct...

GB "Can I please be your slave tonight?"

F « Puis-je être ton esclave ce soir ? »

D „ Darf ich heute Nacht Ihr Sklave sein ? "

I "Posso essere la tua schiava stanotte per favore?"

E "¿Puedo ser tu esclava esta noche?"

P "Por favor, posso ser a sua escrava esta noite?"

S "Snälla, kan jag inte få vara din slav i natt?"

GB "I'll try anything once!"

F «Je suis prête à tout essayer»

D „Ich versuche alles wenigstens einmal."

I "Voglio provare tutto almeno una volta nella vita."

E "Lo probaré todo una vez."

P "Tentarei tudo uma vez."

S "Jag är beredd att pröva allt!"

Direct...

GB "Pardon me, but may I attempt to seduce you?"

F « Excuse-moi mais est-ce que je peux tenter de te séduire ? »

D „ Entschuldigung, kann ich bitte versuchen, Sie zu verführen ? "

I "Mi scusi, potrei provare a sedurla?"

E "Perdona pero ¿puedo intentar seducirte?"

P "Desculpe, mas posso tentar seduzi-lo?"

S "Ursäkta mig, men får jag försöka förföra dig?"

Direct...

GB "Why don't we slip off and see if we can ruin the suspension on my car?"

F « Pourquoi ne pas s'éclipser pour tester les suspensions de ma voiture ? »

D „Warum verschwinden wir hier nicht einfach und sehen ob wir die Stoßdämpfer in meinem Auto ruinieren können. "

I "Perchè non svicoliamo fuori e proviamo a vedere se riusciamo a far saltare le sospensioni della mia macchina?"

E "¿Por qué no nos escapamos y descubrimos si podemos estropear los amortiguadores de mi coche?"

P "Por que é que não damos uma escapadela e vamos ver se conseguimos estragar a suspensão do meu carro?"

S "Jag tycker vi smiter iväg och försöker förstöra min bils fjädring."

Direct...

GB "Would you be interested in a sexual experience which will blow your mind?"

F « Ça te dit une expérience sexuelle qui te fera tourner la tête ? »

D „ Hätten Sie gerne eine sexuelle Begegnung, die Ihnen den Verstand raubt ? "

I "Saresti interessato in un rapporto sessuale che potrebbe farti saltare le cervella?"

E "¿Estarías interesado en una experiencia sexual que te hará alucinar?"

P "Estaria interessado numa experiência sexual que lhe incharia a cabeça?"

S "Skulle du vara intresserad av sexuell extas?"

GB "Are you ready to go home yet?"

F « On rentre, tu es prêt ? »

D „ Sind Sie jetzt fertig zum Gehen ? "

I "Allora sei pronto per andare a casa?"

E "¿Ya estás listo para ir a casa?"

P "Já está pronto para ir para casa?

S "Är det inte dags att vi går hem till dig?"

Direct...

GB "Fancy coming back to my place for breakfast?"

F « Ça te dit de revenir chez moi pour le petit déjeuner ? »

D „ Haben Sie Lust mit zu mir zum Frühstücken zu kommen ? "

I "Vorresti venire a far colazione a casa mia?"

E "¿Te apetece un desayuno en mi casa?"

P "Gostaria de vir a minha casa tomar o pequeno-almoço?"

S "Har du lust att följa med hem till mig och äta frukost?"

GB "There's a 50% chance that we have sex tonight. I want to – do you?"

F « Il y a 50 % de chance pour qu'on couche ensemble ce soir. Moi je le veux ... et toi ? »

D „ Es besteht eine 50% Chance, dass wir heute Nacht miteinander schlafen – ich bin dafür – und Sie ? "

I "C'è un 50% di probabilità che finiremo per fare l'amore stasera: a me sta bene e a te?"

E "Hay un 50% de posibilidades de que nos acostemos juntos esta noche. Yo quiero, ¿y tú?"

P "Há 50% de possibilidade de fazermos sexo esta noite. Eu quero – e tu?"

S "Det finns en 50-procentig chans att vi kommer att älska ikväll. Jag vill – vill du?"

Direct...

GB "I had a really sexy dream last night, and you were the star. I want to know if you are that good in reality."

F « J'ai fait un rêve très érotique la nuit dernière et tu en étais la star. Je veux savoir si c'est vrai. »

D „ Letzte Nacht hatte ich einen sehr erotischen Traum, und Sie waren der Star. Ich möchte gern wissen, ob Sie auch in der Wirklichkeit so gut sind. "

I "Stanotte ho fatto un sogno erotico e tu ne eri il protagonista. Voglio sapere se anche nella realtà sei veramente così bravo."

E "Tuve un sueño muy sexy la noche anterior y tú eras la estrella. Me encantaría saber si en realidad eres tan bueno."

P "Tive um sonho erótico na noite passada, e tu eras a estrela. Quero saber se és de facto tão bom na realidade."

S "Jag drömde en riktigt sexig dröm i natt och du hade huvudrollen. Jag vill ta reda på om du är så bra i verkligheten."

Direct...

GB "You know, you look a lot like my next boyfriend."

F « Tu sais que tu ressembles beaucoup à mon prochain petit ami ? »

D „Kaum zu glauben, Sie sehen aus wie mein nächster Liebhaber."

I "Sai che assomigli un sacco al mio futuro ragazzo?"

E "Sabes, te pareces mucho a mi próximo novio."

P "Você é muito parecido com o meu próximo namorado."

S "Du är väldigt lik min blivande pojkvän."

Direct...

GB "Your place or mine?"

F « Chez toi ou chez moi ? »

D „Ihre Wohnung oder meine ? "

I "Da te o da me?"

E "¿Tu casa o la mía?"

P "Na tua casa ou na minha?"

S "Hem till dig eller mig?"

GB "Get your coat... You've scored!"

F « Touché ! Prends ton manteau ! »

D „Nehmen Sie Ihren Mantel – Sie hatten Glück."

I "Prendi il cappotto... mi hai stregato!"

E "Coge el abrigo... Has ligado."

P "Apanhe o seu casaco..."

S "Hämta din jacka...du har fått napp!"

Direct...

GB "How about a night of passion in [your town]?"

F « Ça te dirait une nuit passionnée à [votre ville]? »

D „Wie wär's mit einer Nacht voller Leidenschaft in ... (ihre Stadt)"

I "Che cosa ne pensi di una notte di fuoco a [e qui devi menzionare il nome della tua città]?"

E "¿Qué tal una noche de pasión en [tu ciudad]?"

P "Que tal uma noite de paixão na [cidade dele]."

S "Vad sägs om en het natt i [din stad]?"

GB "I don't want to know your name, just make love to me!"

F «Je ne veux pas connaître ton nom, fais-moi l'amour!»

D „Ich habe nicht nach Ihrem Namen gefragt, lassen Sie uns einfach ins Bett gehen."

I "Non voglio sapere come ti chiami, fammi l'amore e basta."

E "No quiero saber cómo te llamas. Limítate a hacerme el amor."

P "Não quero saber o seu nome, faça apenas amor comigo."

S "Jag vill inte veta vad du heter, älska bara med mig!"

Direct...

GB "I think I'm falling in love with you. Now, do you want to make love?"

F «Je crois que je suis amoureuse. Bon, tu veux faire l'amour ? »

D „ Ich glaube, ich verliebe mich in Sie. Können wir jetzt ins Bett ? "

I "Penso di essermi innamorata di te. E adesso sei pronto a fare l'amore?"

E "Creo que me estoy enamorando de ti. Y ahora, ¿quieres acostarte conmigo?"

P "Penso que estou a apaixonar por si. Assim sendo, quer fazer amor?"

S "Jag tror jag håller på att bli kär i dig. Vill du älska nu då?"

Direct...

GB "I'll show you mine if you'll show me yours."

F « Je te les montre si tu me les montre . »

D „ Ich zeige Ihnen meines, wenn Sie mir Ihres zeigen. "

I "Ti faccio vedere la mia, se mi fai vedere il tuo."

E "Te enseñaré el mío, si tú me enseñas el tuyo."

P "Eu mostro-lhe a minha e você mostra-me a sua."

S "Jag visar min om du visar din."

Direct...

GB "Your place or the men's bathroom?"

F « Chez toi ou dans les toilettes des hommes? »

D „ Ihre Wohnung oder die Herrentoilette ? "

I "Da te o nel bagno degli uomini?"

E "¿Tu casa o el lavabo de caballeros?"

P "Em sua casa ou na casa de banho dos homens?"

S "Hemma hos dig eller inne på herrtoaletten?"

GB "Hope you've got your toothbrush, you'll need it."

F « J'espère que tu as ta brosse à dents car tu va en avoir besoin. »

D „Ich hoffe Sie haben Ihre Zahnbürste dabei, Sie werden sie brauchen."

I "Spero che ti sia portato lo spazzolino da denti perchè ne avrai bisogno."

E "Espero que hayas cogido tu cepillo de dientes, te hará falta."

P "Espero que tenhas trazido a escova de dentes, vais precisar dela."

S "Hoppas du har med dig tandborsten, du kommer att behöva den."

Direct...

GB "How about coming back to my place for a spot of heavy breathing?"

F « Ça te dit d'aller chez moi pour un quart d'heure haletant ? »

D „Was halten Sie davon, mit zu mir zu kommen ? Wir können ein wenig zusammen Stöhnen. "

I "Che cosa ne dici se andiamo da me per una sessione di gemiti e sospiri?"

E "¿Qué tal venirte a mi casa para una sesión de jadeo?"

P "Que tal irmos até minha casa para um pouco de respiração ofegante?"

S "Vad sägs om att följa med mig hem och stöna lite?"

Direct...

GB "What do you like for breakfast?"

F « Qu'est ce que tu aimes au petit déjeuner? »

D „Was frühstücken Sie gern?"

I "Che cosa ti piace mangiare a colazione?"

E "¿Qué desayunas?"

P "O que é que quer para o pequeno-almoço?"

S "Vad vill du ha till frukost?"

Direct...

GB "Will it bother you when I sleep in the nude?"

F « Ça t'embête pas si je dors nue? »

D „Stört es Sie, wenn ich nackt schlafe?"

I "Ti dà fastidio se dormo nuda?"

E "¿Te molestaré si duermo desnuda?"

P "Incomodava-o se eu dormisse nua?"

S "Kommer det att störa dig när jag sover naken?"

Humorous...

Humorous...

GB "Strawberry, chocolate or ribbed? the choice is yours."

F « Fraise, chocolat ou napolitaine ? Choisis. »

D „Erdbeere, Schokolade oder gerippelt ? Ihre Wahl."

I "Fragola, cioccolato o lubrificato: a te la scelta."

E "¿De fresa, chocolate o con relieve? La decisión es tuya."

P "Morangos, chocolate ou costelas? A escolha é sua."

S "Jordgubb, choklad eller knottrig? Valet är ditt."

GB "Think of a number between 1 and 10. You lose – take your clothes off!"

F «Choisis un chiffre entre 1 et 10... Perdu ! Déshabille-toi!»

D „Denken Sie an eine Zahl zwischen 1 und 10. Sie haben verloren – ziehen Sie sich aus"

I "Pensa a un numero da 1 a 100. Hai perso – spogliati!"

E "Piensa un número del 1 al 10. Has perdido. Sácate la ropa."

P "Pense num número entre 1 e 10. Perdeu – dispa-se!"

S "Tänk på ett nummer mellan 1 och 10. Fel – ta av dig kläderna!"

Humorous...

GB "Hi, I just wanted to give you the satisfaction of turning me down. Go ahead, say no."

F « Salut, je voulais juste te donner le plaisir de me repousser. Allez, dit moi non ! »

D „ Hallo, ich wollte Ihnen nur die Gelegenheit geben, mich abzulehnen. Machen Sie schon, sagen Sie nein. "

I "Ciao, volevo solamente darti la soddisfazione di respingermi. Avanti, dì di no!"

E "Hola. Sólo quería darte la satisfacción de rechazarme. Venga, di que no."

P "Olá, quero apenas dar-te o prazer de me rejeitares. Vá lá, diz não."

S "Hej, jag ville bara ge dig tillfredsställelsen att rata mig. Kom igen, säg nej."

Humorous...

GB "I've got the body of a model... she's buried under the patio back home."

F « J'ai le corps d'un top model...elle et enterrée dans mon patio. »

D „ Ich habe den Körper eines Modells... sie liegt Zuhause unter der Terrasse. "

I "Ho il corpo di una fotomodella ... è sotterrato nel mio giardino di casa."

E "Tengo el cuerpo de una modelo... está enterrada en el patio de mi casa."

P "Tenho o corpo de uma modelo... está enterrada no pátio das traseiras da minha casa."

S "Jag har en mannekängs kropp...den ligger begravd under verandan hemma."

Humorous...

GB "What is a nice guy like you doing in a dirty mind like mine?"

F « Qu'est-ce qu'un beau mec comme toi fait dans un esprit aussi mal tourné que le mien ? »

D „Was macht ein netter Mann wie Sie in einer schmutzigen Phantasie wie meiner ? "

I "Che cosa ci fa un ragazzo così dolce nei miei pensieri così sporchi?"

E "¿Qué hace un buen chico como tú en una mente tan verde como la mía?"

P "O que é que um tipo bonito como tu está a fazer numa cabeça suja como a minha?"

S "Vad gör en fin kille som du i min snuskiga fantasi?"

Humorous...

GB "Excuse me do you live around here often?"

F « Excusez-moi, vous traînez souvent dans les parages ? »

D „Entschuldigung, leben Sie hier oft ? "

I "Mi scusi, ma abita spesso da queste parti?"

E "Disculpa ¿vives por aquí a menudo?"

P "Desculpa, mas vives aqui perto frequentemente?"

S "Ursäkta mig, bor du ofta i närheten?"

Humorous...

GB "My son is a cold hearted gangster, and I need a hug."

F « Mon fils est un gangster au sang-froid et j'ai besoin d'un câlin. »

D „ Mein Sohn ist ein kaltschnäuziger Gangster und ich brauche eine Umarmung. "

I "Mio figlio è un gangster senza cuore e ho tanto bisogno di coccole."

E "Mi hijo es un gángster sin corazón, y yo necesito un abrazo."

P "O meu filho é um gangster frio e implacável, e eu preciso de um abraço."

S "Min son är en kallblodig gangster och jag behöver en kram."

Humorous...

GB "They call me the Mouth of God, and not because I talk well."

F « On m'appelle bouche divine mais c'est pas parce que je parle bien. »

D „Man nennt mich den Mund Gottes, aber nicht, weil ich gut reden kann."

I "Mi chiamano la Bocca di Dio, e non è perchè parlo bene."

E "Me llaman la boca de Dios y no es porque hable bien."

P "Chamam-me Boca de Deus, mas não por causa da maneira de falar."

S "De kallar mig guds mun och det är inte för att jag är välartikulerad."

Humorous...

GB "£20 says I can make you the happiest man on earth tonight."

F «Avec 200 francs je parie que tu seras l'homme le plus heureux de la terre ce soir.»

D „Ich wette 20 Mark, dass ich Sie zum glücklichsten Mann der Welt machen kann."

I "£50.000 mi dicono che stasera farò di te l'uomo più felice del mondo."

E "Apuesto 4000 pesetas a que puedo hacerte el hombre más feliz de la tierra esta noche."

P "Aposto 500 escudos em como posso fazer de ti esta noite o homem mais feliz do mundo."

S "200 spänn på att jag kan göra dig världens lyckligaste man i kväll."

Humorous...

GB "Hey big boy, do you want to see some puppies?"

F « Eh beau mec, tu veux voir des puppies ? »

D „Hallo mein Süßer, möchten Sie junge Hündchen sehen ? "

I "Ehi, bel maschione, vorresti vedere la mia farfallina?"

E "Hola guapo, ¿quieres ver unos peluches?"

P "Ei machão, queres ter alguns filhotes?"

S "Hej, vill du se några meloner?"

Humorous...

GB "Hi, the voices in my head told me to come over here and talk to you!"

F «Salut ! Mes voix me disent de venir ici et de parler.»

D „Hallo, die Stimmen in meinem Kopf haben mir befohlen herzukommen und mit Ihnen zu sprechen."

I "Ciao, le voci che sento nella mia testa mi hanno suggerito di venire qui a parlare con te."

E "Hola. Hay voces en mi cabeza que me dicen que venga aquí a hablarte."

P "Olá, as vozes da minha cabeça disseram-me para vir aqui e falar contigo."

S "Hej, rösterna i mitt huvud sa till mig att gå hit och prata med dig."

Humorous...

GB "If l were to ask you for sex, would your answer be the same as the answer to this question?"

F « Si je te demande de coucher avec moi, est-ce que ta réponse sera la même que la réponse à cette question ? »

D „Wenn ich Sie um Sex bitten würde, wäre Ihre Antwort die Gleiche, wie die Antwort auf diese Frage ? "

I "Se ti chiedessi di fare del sesso, la tua risposta sarebbe come la risposta a questa domanda?"

E "Si te pidiera que nos acostáramos juntos ¿responderías igual que a esta pregunta?"

P "Se eu te pedisse sexo, a tua resposta seria a mesma que a resposta a esta pergunta?"

S "Om jag skulle fråga om du ville älska, skulle ditt svar vara det samma som svaret på den här frågan?"

Humorous...

GB "If I weren't so romantic, I'd shoot you."

F « Si je n'étais pas si romantique, je te tirerai dessus. »

D „Wenn ich nicht so romantisch wäre, würde ich auf Sie schießen. "

I "Se non fossi così romantica, ti sparerei."

E "Si no fuera tan romántica, te pegaría un tiro."

P "Se eu não fosse tão romântica, matava-te."

S "Om jag inte vore så kär skulle jag skjuta dig."

Humorous...

GB "My eyes seem small but I've got a huge personality."

F « Mes yeux ont l'air petit mais j'ai une très grande personnalité. »

D „ Meine Augen erscheinen vielleicht sehr klein, ich habe aber eine große Persönlichkeit "

I "I miei occhi sembrano piccoli, ma ho una personalità enorme."

E "Mis ojos parecen pequeños, pero tengo una gran personalidad."

P "Os meus olhos parecem pequenos mas tenho uma personalidade profunda."

S "Mina ögon verkar små men jag har en enorm personlighet."

Humorous...

GB "You're so hot, you're melting my rubber g-string!"

F « Il fait si chaud près de toi que mon string en latex est en train de fondre »

D „Sie sind so heiß, dass meine Gummi-Reizwäsche schmilzt."

I "Sei così bollente che il mio perizoma si sta sciogliendo!

E "Estás tan bueno que se me derriten las gomas del tanga."

P "És tão quente... Estás a derreter a minha tanga de borracha."

S "Du är så het att mina gummitrosor håller på att smälta

Humorous...

GB "I think you are totally awesome. I want to marry you. Please don't tell my boyfriend."

F « Je te trouve génial. J'ai envie de me marier avec toi. S'il te plaît, ne dis rien à mon petit ami. »

D „Ich finde Sie völlig irre. Ich will Sie heiraten. Bitte sagen Sie meinem Freund nichts davon."

I "Penso che sei favoloso. Voglio sposarti. Ma per favore non dirlo al mio ragazzo!"

E "Eres imponente. Quiero casarme contigo. Por favor, no se lo digas a mi novio."

P "Penso que és um verdadeiro espanto. Quero casar contigo. Por favor, não digas ao meu namorado."

S "Jag tycker att du är otrolig. Jag vill gifta mig med dig. Snälla, säg inget till min pojkvän."

Humorous...

GB "OK, you can stand next to me as long as you don't talk about the temperature."

F « D'accord, tu peux rester près de moi tant que tu ne parles pas de la chaleur qu'il fait ici. »

D „ Ok, Sie können neben mir stehen, solange Sie die Temperatur nicht erwähnen. "

I "Va bene, puoi sederti vicino a me, a patto che non menzioni la temperatura."

E "Vale, puedes quedarte a mi lado, siempre que no hables sobre la temperatura."

P "Está bem, podes ficar ao pé de mim desde que não te queixes da temperatura."

S "OK, du får stå bredvid mig bara du inte talar om vädre

Humorous...

GB "Since we shouldn't waste things in this day and age, let's use these condoms in my pocket before they expire."

F « Puisqu'il ne faut pas perdre de temps de nos jours, utilisons les préservatifs qui sont dans ma poche avant qu'ils n'arrivent à expiration. »

D „ Heutzutage sollte man eigentlich nichts vergeuden. Lassen Sie uns meine Kondome benutzen, bevor sie zu alt und brüchig werden. "

I "Dal momento che non dobbiamo sprecare niente di questi tempi, perchè non finiamo i preservativi che ho in tasca prima che scadono?"

E "Ya que hoy en día no se deben derrochar las cosas, aprovechemos los condones que llevo en el bolsillo antes de que caduquen."

P "Uma vez que não devemos desperdiçar nada nestes dias e nesta época, vamos usar estas camisinhas que tenho no bolso antes que expirem."

S "Eftersom man inte bör slösa med saker och ting i dessa dagar, så är det bäst att vi använder dessa kondomer innan bäst-före datum."

Humorous...

GB "Take me to bed or lose me for ever."

F «Prends moi dans ton lit ou perds moi à jamais.»

D „Gehen Sie mit mir ins Bett oder Sie verlieren mich für immer."

I "Portami a letto subito o mi perderai per sempre."

E "Llévame a la cama o piérdeme para siempre."

P "Leva-me para a cama ou perdes-me para sempre."

S "För mig i säng eller förlora mig för alltid."

Humorous...

GB "Wow! Are you really as beautiful as you seem, or do you just remind me of myself?"

F « Ouah ! Tu es si beau que ça ou est-ce que tu me ressembles ? »

D „ Wow, – Sind Sie wirklich so schön, oder erinnern Sie mich einfach nur an mich selbst ? "

I "Uao! Sei veramente così bello come sembri, o è solo perchè assomigli così tanto a me?"

E "¡Caramba! ¿Eres tan guapo como pareces o sólo me recuerdas a mi misma?"

P "Uau! És realmente tão belo como pareces, ou apenas fazes-me recordar a mim mesma?"

S "Wow! Är du verkligen så snygg som du verkar eller påminner du mig bara om mig själv?"

Humorous...

GB "Can you believe it? It's been more than fifteen minutes since I've had sex."

F « Est-ce que tu te rends compte que ça fait plus d'un quart d'heure que j'ai fait l'amour ? »

D „ Es ist kaum zu glauben, es ist jetzt schon mehr als fünfzehn Minuten her, seitdem ich das letzte Mal mit jemandem geschlafen habe. "

I "Ci credi che non faccio l'amore da più di un quarto d'ora?"

E "¿Puedes creerlo? Ya hace más de quince minutos que no me llevo a nadie a la cama."

P "Acreditas nisto? Já se passaram mais de quinze minutos desde tive relações sexuais?"

S "Kan du tänka dig? Det har gått mer än femton minuter sedan jag senast hade sex."

Humorous...

GB "I'm not trying anything. I always put my hands there."

F « Je n'essaie rien du tout. Je mets toujours mes mains là. »

D „Ich mache gar nichts, ich habe meine Hände immer dort. "

I "Non sto provandoci per niente. Metto sempre le mani in quel posto."

E "No estoy intentando nada. Siempre pongo mis manos aquí."

P "Não estou a tentar nada. Eu sempre pus ali as mãos."

S "Jag försöker inte med någonting. Jag lägger alltid mina händer där."

Humorous...

GB "I've got one hour to live and don't want to die a virgin. Help me."

F « Il me reste une heure à vivre et je ne veux pas mourir vierge. Aidez-moi. »

D „ Ich habe nur noch eine Stunde zu leben und will nichts als Jungfrau sterben. Bitte helfen Sie mir. "

I "Ho solamente un'ora di vita e non voglio morire vergine. Aiutami!"

E "Me queda una hora de vida y no quiero morir virgen. ¡Ayúdame!"

P "Tenho uma hora para viver e não quero morrer virgem. Ajude-me."

S "Jag har en timme kvar att leva och jag vill inte dö oskuld. Hjälp mig."

Humorous...

GB "You've heard of 'See no evil' and 'Hear no evil'. I'm 'I don't talk with my mouth full'!"

F « Tu as entendu parler de "ne rien écouter de mauvais" et de "rien regarder de mauvais" ? Eh bien moi on m'appelle "ne parle pas la bouche pleine". »

D „Haben Sie schon von den drei Affen gehört : Nichts sehen, nichts hören....Ich bin : Sprich nicht mit vollem Mund. "

I "Hai già sentito dire 'parla come mangi' e 'mangia con la bocca chiusa'. Il mio motto è 'non parlare con la bocca piena'."

E "¿Sabes lo de 'no ver, no oír'? Pues yo no hablo con la boca llena."

P "Diz-se 'Não ver o mal' e 'Não ouvir o mal'. Eu prefiro 'Não falo com a boca cheia'!"

S "Jag har alltid lärt mig att man inte skall tala med munnen full."

Humorous...

GB "I bet you'd love to see my brass rubbings?"

F « Je parie que tu adorerais voir mes estampes japonaises. »

D „ Ich wette, dass Sie meine Kunststücke sehen wollen. "

I "Scommetto che daresti chissà cosa per vedere come funziona la mia pompa."

E "Apuesto a que te encantaría probar mis dotes de masajista."

P "Aposto que gostarias de ver os meus bronzes polidos."

S "Jag slår vad om att du skulle vilja se min vykortssamling."

Humorous...

GB "Wouldn't we look cute on a wedding cake together?"

F « On ne serait pas mignons sur un gâteau de mariage tous les deux ? »

D „ Wir würden toll nebeneinander auf einer Hochtzeitstorte aussehen. "

I "Non saremmo carini su una torta nuziale?"

E "¡Qué bien quedaríamos encima de un pastel de boda!"

P "Não ficaríamos giros juntos num bolo de noiva?"

S "Skulle vi inte se söta ut på en bröllopstårta tillsammans?"

Humorous...

GB   "You've been a bad boy! Go to my room!"

F   « Méchant garçon ! File dans ma chambre ! »

D   „Sie waren ein schlechter Junge. Gehen Sie sofort auf mein Zimmer. "

I   "Sei stato cattivo! Vai nella mia camera!"

E   "Has sido un chico malo. ¡Vete a mi habitación!"

P   "Tens sido um menino mal-comportado! Já para o meu quarto!"

S   "Du har varit en stygg pojke! Gå till mitt rum!"

Insulting...

Insulting...

GB "Correct me if I'm wrong, but is that a Wonderbra you've got on?"

F « Dites moi si je me trompe, mais c'est un Wonderbra que vous portez ? »

D „ Ich kann mich ja auch irren, aber ist das nicht ein Wonderbra, den Sie da tragen ? "

I "Correggimi pure se sbaglio, ma non indossi per caso un reggiseno imbottito?"

E "Corrígeme si me equivoco pero ¿no es un Wonderbra eso que llevas?"

P "Corrija-me se estou enganada, mas você está a usar um soutiã com chumaços?"

S "Rätta mig om jag har fel, men är inte det där en pushup du har på dig?"

Insulting...

"I like a dangerous fool... so are you out on bail?"

«J'aime bien les gros dangereux...on t'a libéré sous caution?»

„Ich mag gefährliche Männer... sind Sie auf Bewährung draußen?"

"Mi piacciono gli idioti pericolosi ... sei per caso in libertà provvisoria?"

"Me gustan los locos peligrosos... ¿así que has salido bajo fianza, eh?"

"Gosto de um louco perigoso... você está cá fora em liberdade condicional?"

"Jag gillar farliga idioter...har du frisläppts nyligen, eller?"

Insulting...

GB "If I said you have an ugly body, would you hold it against me?"

F « Si je te dis que ton corps est très laid, tu te presseras tout contre moi ? »

D „Wenn ich sagen würde dass Sie einen häßlichen Körper haben, würden Sie das gegen mich verwenden ? "

I "Se ti dicessi che hai un brutto corpo, lo useresti contro di me?"

E "Si te dijera que tienes un cuerpo feo ¿lo apretujarías contra el mío?"

P "Se eu dissesse que tinhas um corpo feito, atiravas-te com ele para cima de mim?"

S "Du är ful och jag är full, men i morgon är jag nykter..."

Insulting...

GB "What's a nice guy like you doing with a face like that?"

F « Qu'est ce qu'un gentil gars comme toi fait avec un visage pareil ? »

D „ Was macht ein netter Mann wie Sie mit solch einem häßlichen Gesicht ? "

I "Che cosa ci fà un ragazzo così simpatico con una faccia come la tua?"

E "¿Qué hace un chico bueno como tú con una cara tan fea como ésta?"

P "O que é que um tipo giro como tu faz com uma cara dessas?"

S "Vad gör en snäll kille som du med ett ansikte som ditt?"

Insulting...

GB "What's an idiot like you doing in a good bar like this?"

F « Qu'est-ce qu'un idiot comme toi fait dans ce bar ? »

D „Was macht ein Idiot wie Sie in einer guten Kneipe wie dieser ? "

I "Che cosa ci fà un poco di buono come te in questo bar così per bene?"

E "¿Qué hace un idiota como tú en un bar tan bueno como éste?"

P "O que é que um idiota como tu faz num bar tão bom como este?"

S "Vad gör en nolla som du på en bra bar som denna?"

Insulting...

GB "You don't smell too bad for a fat bloke."

F « Tu ne sens pas trop mauvais pour un gros tas. »

D „Für einen fetten Mann stinken Sie gar nicht so schlimm."

I "Non puzzi tanto per essere così grasso."

E "Para lo gordo que eres, no hueles mal."

P "Você não cheira assim tão mal para um tipo gordo."

S "Du luktar inte så illa för att vara så fet."

Insulting...

GB "Everyone is beautiful in the dark – even you."

F « Dans le noir tout le monde est beau, même toi. »

D „Jeder ist schöner im Dunklen – sogar Sie. "

I "Tutti siamo belli al buio – anche tu."

E "Todo el mundo es guapo en la oscuridad, incluido tú."

P "Toda a gente é bonita no escuro – até tu."

S "Alla är vackra i mörkret – till och med du."

Insulting...

GB "I love a guy who's not ashamed to be a slob."

F « J'adore les types qui n'ont pas honte d'être des ploucs ! »

D „ Ich mag Männer die sich nicht schämen schlampig auszusehen. "

I "Amo l'uomo che non si vergogna di essere sciattone."

E "Me gustan los tíos que no se avergüenzan de ser patanes."

P "Gosto de um tipo que não tenha vergonha de ser um estúpido."

S "Jag älskar killar som inte skäms över att vara sluskar."

Insulting...

GB "I've had quite a bit to drink and you're beginning to look pretty good!"

F « C'est vrai qu'après quelques verres tu commences à être très mignon ! »

D „ Ich habe schon eine ganze Menge getrunken, und langsam sehen Sie ganz gut aus. "

I "Ho bevuto un po' troppo e sto cominciando a pensare che sei carino."

E "He bebido un poco y estás empezando a parecerme bastante potable."

P "Já bebi um bocado e você começa a parecer-me bastante melhor."

S "Jag har druckit en hel del och du börjar se ganska bra ut."

Insulting...

GB "You smell. Want to take a shower together?"

F « Tu ne sens pas bon. Ça te dit de prendre une douche avec moi ? »

D „ Sie stinken, wollen Sie mit mir duschen ? "

I "Puzzi. Vuoi fare una doccia con me?"

E "Hueles. ¿Nos duchamos juntos?"

P "Cheiras mal. Tomamos banho juntos?"

S "Du luktar. Vill du duscha med mig?"

Insulting...

GB "I know a sleazy motel with a cheap hourly rate. It woul suit you."

F « Je connais un motel miteux où le tarif horaire est bon marché. Ça t'irait parfaitement. »

D „ Ich kenne da 'ne schreckliche Absteige, mit billigen Stundenmieten. Wäre genau das Richtige für Sie. "

I "Conosco un motel malfamato e a poco prezzo." propri adatto a te."

E "Conozco un motel asqueroso a un precio por horas mu barato. Ideal para ti."

P "Conheço um motel pobre com preços baratos à hora. É que te serve."

S "Jag känner till ett sjaskigt motell med billig timtaxa. D skulle passa dig."

Insulting...

GB "I know a great way to burn some of those calories off your beer-belly."

F « Je connais un excellent moyen pour brûler les calories de cette bedaine pleine de bière. »

D „Ich kenne da eine großartige Methode das Fett von Ihrem Bierbauch loszuwerden."

I "Conosco una maniera perfetta per bruciare un po' di calorie da quella pancia che ti ritrovi."

E "Conozco un método fantástico para quemar esas calorías de tu barriga."

P "Sei de uma óptima maneira de queimar as calorias da tua barriga de cerveja."

S "Jag vet ett perfekt sätt att bli av med din ölmage."

Insulting...

GB "God, with a face like that no wonder your hands are rough!"

F « Oh la, la, avec une tête pareille, pas étonnant que tes mains soient si rugueuses ! »

D „ Mensch, mit einem Gesicht wie Ihrem überrascht es mich nicht, dass Ihre Hände so rauh sind. "

I "O Gesù, con una faccia come la tua non c'è da meravigliarsi che hai le mani così rozze!"

E "Tio, con una cara como esa no me extraña que tengas callos en las manos."

P "Deus, com uma cara como essa não admira que as tua mãos estejam ásperas."

S "Herregud, med ett ansikte som ditt är det inte konstigt att du har så grova händer!"

Insulting...

GB "You're ugly but you intrigue me."

F « Ta laideur m'intrigue »

D „Sie sind so häßlich, dass ich Sie interessant finde. "

I "Sei brutto ma mi affascini."

E "Eres feo pero me intrigas."

P "Tu és feio mas intrigas-me."

S "Du är ful, men du fängslar mig."

Romantic...

Romantic...

GB "If I followed you home looking lost, would you give me a bed for the night?"

F « Si je vous suis chez vous avec un air de chien battu, est-ce que vous me donnerez un lit pour la nuit ? »

D „ Wenn ich Ihnen nachlaufen würde und hilflos aussähe, würden Sie mich bei sich schlafen lassen ? "

I "Se ti seguissi fino a casa con l'aria sperduta, mi daresti un letto per la notte?"

E "Si te siguiera a casa pareciendo perdida ¿me ofrecerías una cama para pasar la noche?"

P "Se o seguisse até casa com ar de perdida, dava-me cama por uma noite?"

S "Om jag följde med dig hem och såg vilsen ut, skulle du då erbjuda mig en säng för natten?"

Romantic...

GB "Don't worry about it. Nothing that you've ever done before counts. The only thing that matters now is that we're together."

F « Ne vous inquiétez pas. Ce que vous avez fait avant ne compte pas. La seule chose qui compte aujourd'hui c'est que nous sommes ensemble. »

D „ Machen Sie sich nichts draus. Nichts, was Sie bisher gemacht haben zählt. Das einzig Wichtige ist, dass wir jetzt zusammen sind. "

I "Non preoccuparti. Quello che hai fatto prima non conta niente per me. L'unica cosa che conta è che adesso siamo insieme."

E "No te preocupes. Nada de lo que hayas hecho en tu pasado cuenta. Lo único que importa ahora es que estamos juntos."

P "Não se preocupe. Nada do que tenha feito antes conta. A única coisa que conta agora é que estamos aqui juntos."

S "Oroa dig inte för det. Inget som hänt förr spelar någon roll. Det enda som betyder något nu är att vi är tillsammans."

Romantic...

GB "Excuse me, do you mind if I stare at you for a minute? I want to remember your face for my dreams."

F « Excusez-moi, ça ne vous embête pas que je vous observe une minute ? Je veux me souvenir de votre visage pour mes rêves. »

D „ Entschuldigung, stört es Sie, wenn ich Sie eine Weile anstarre ? Ich möchte mir Ihr Gesicht einprägen damit ich davon träumen kann. "

I "Mi scusi, ma le dà fastidio se la fisso per un momento? Voglio ricordarmi il suo viso nei miei sogni."

E "Discúlpame ¿te importa si te miro un rato? Quiero recordar tu cara en mis sueños."

P "Desculpe, importa-se que o contemple durante um minuto? Quero recordar a sua cara nos meus sonhos."

S "Ursäkta mig, tar du illa upp om jag stirrar på dig en stund? Jag vill komma ihåg hur du ser ut när jag drömmer i kväll."

Romantic...

GB "If you take my heart by surprise, don't you think the rest of my body has a right to follow?"

F « Si vous prenez mon cœur par surprise, ne croyez-vous pas que le reste de mon corps a le droit de suivre ? »

D „Wenn Sie mein Herz so überraschend stehlen, warum sollte mein Körper dann nicht folgen ? "

I "Dal momento che hai preso il mio cuore di sopresa, non credi che anche il resto del mio corpo ha diritto alla stesso trattamento?"

E "Si me has tomado el corazón por sorpresa ¿no crees que el resto de mi cuerpo tiene el derecho a seguirlo?"

P "Se te apoderares do meu coração de surpresa, não achas que o resto do meu corpo tem o direito de ir também?"

S "Om du lurar med dig mitt hjärta tycker du då inte att min kropp har rätt att få följa med?"

Romantic...

GB "Now I understand why the sky has been grey all day – all the blue is in your eyes!"

F « Maintenant je comprends pourquoi il a fait gris toute la journée : tout le bleu est dans vos yeux ! »

D „Jetzt weiß ich auch, warum der Himmel den ganzen Tag so grau war, alles blau ist in Ihren Augen."

I "Adesso capisco perchè il cielo era così grigio oggi – tutto l'azzurro è nei tuoi occhi!"

E "Ahora entiendo por qué el cielo ha estado gris todo el día. Todo el azul está en tus ojos!"

P "Agora compreendo por que razão o céu tem estado cinzento todo o dia – o azul está todo nos teus olhos!"

S "Nu vet jag varför himlen varit grå hela dagen...allt det blå finns i dina ögon."

Romantic...

GB "There must be something wrong with my eyes. I can't take them off you!"

F « Je dois avoir un problème de vue. Je n'arrive pas à vous quitter des yeux ! »

D „ Irgend etwas stimmt mit meinen Augen nicht, ich kann sie einfach nicht von Ihnen lassen. "

I "Deve esserci qualcosa di strano con i miei occhi. Non riesco a toglierteli di dosso!"

E "No sé que les pasa a mis ojos. No puedo dejar de mirarte."

P "Deve haver qualquer coisa errada com os meus olhos. Não consigo afastá-los de ti!"

S "Det måste vara något fel på mina ögon. Jag kan inte lämna dig med blicken."

Romantic...

GB "What can I do to make you mine?"

F « Qu'est-ce que je dois faire pour que vous soyez à moi ? »

D „ Was muss ich tun, damit Sie der Meine werden ? "

I "Cosa devo fare per farti mio?"

E "¿Qué puedo hacer para que seas mío?"

P "O que posso fazer para que sejas minha?"

S "Vad skall jag göra för att du skall bli min?"

Romantic...

GB "If you say no, you'll regret it. Maybe not today, maybe not tomorrow, but some day, and for the rest of your life."

F « Si vous dites non, vous le regretterez. Peut-être pas aujourd'hui, peut-être pas demain, mais peut-être un jour, et jusqu'à la fin de vos jours. »

D „Wenn Sie jetzt nein sagen, werden Sie es bereuen. Vielleicht nicht heute, vielleicht auch morgen nicht, aber eines Tages und dann für den Rest Ihres Lebens. "

I "Se mi dici di no, te ne pentirai. Forse non oggi, forse non domani, ma qualche giorno te ne pentirai e sarà per il resto della tua vita."

E "Si dices que no, te arrepentirás. Quizá no hoy, ni mañana, pero algún día y durante el resto de toda tu vida."

P "Se disseres que não, arrependes-te. Hoje, talvez não, talvez não amanhã, mas algum dia, e para o resto da tua vida."

S "Om du säger nej kommer du att ångra dig. Kanske inte idag eller i morgon, men en dag och då blir det för resten av ditt liv."

Romantic...

GB "Can you catch? I think I'm falling for you."

F « Vous voulez bien me rattraper ? Je crois que je tombe amoureuse. »

D „Können Sie gut fangen? Ich glaube ich falle Ihnen zu Füßen. "

I "Sei capace di prendere le cose al volo? Credo che sto per caderti ai piedi."

E "¿Me coges? Me tiemblan las piernas con sólo verte."

P "Agarras-me? Acho que estou a ficar caída por ti."

S "Är du bra på att fånga? Jag tror jag faller för dig."

Romantic...

GB "Do you have a map? I just got lost in your eyes."

F «Vous avez un plan? Je viens de me perdre dans vos yeux.»

D „Haben Sie eine Landkarte? Ich verirre mich in Ihren Augen."

I "Hai una cartina? Mi sono appena persa nei tuoi occhi."

E "¿Tienes un mapa? Acabo de perderme en tus ojos."

P "Tens um mapa? Acabo de me perder nos teue olhos."

S "Har du en karta? Jag gick just vilse i dina ögon."

Romantic...

GB "I've lost that loving feeling. Please help me find it."

F «J'ai perdu le sentiment de l'amour. Vous voulez bien m'aider à le retrouver?»

D „Ich habe das Gefühl der Liebe verloren. Können Sie mir beim Suchen helfen?"

I "Ho perso il senso dell'amore. Per favore aiutami a ritrovarlo."

E "He perdido ese sentimiento de amor. Por favor, ayúdame a encontrarlo."

P "Perdi aquele sentimento amoroso. Por favor ajuda-me a encontrá-lo."

S "Jag har tappat kärleken. Snälla, hjälp mig hitta den."

Romantic...

GB "There must be a rainbow nearby, because you're the treasure I've been searching for."

F « Il doit y avoir un arc-en-ciel près d'ici parce que vous êtes le trésor que je cherche. »

D „ Dies muss das Ende des Regenbogens sein, ich habe endlich den Schatz gefunden, nach dem ich gesucht habe. "

I "Ci deve essere l'arcobaleno da qualche parte, perchè sei il tesoro che stavo cercando."

E "Debe haber un arco iris por aquí, porque tú eres el tesoro que he estado buscando."

P "Deve haver um arco-íris aqui perto, porque tu és o tesouro de que tenho andado à procura."

S "Det måste finnas en regnbåge i närheten, för du är skatten jag har letat efter."

Romantic...

GB "So, what do you do when you're not turning me to jelly?"

F « Qu'est-ce que vous faites dans la vie à part me faire fondre de plaisir ? »

D „ So, was machen Sie, wenn Sie mich nicht gerade in Wackelpudding verwandeln ? "

I "Allora dimmi che cosa fai quando non sei impegnato a farmi perdere la testa."

E "Bueno, ¿y a qué te dedicas cuando no me dejas como un flan?"

P "O que fazes quando não me estás a transformar em geleia?"

S "Så vad sysslar du med när du inte gör mig knäsvag?"

Romantic...

GB "When I look into your eyes I see the moon and the stars."

F « Quand je regarde vos yeux je vois la lune et les étoiles. »

D „Wenn ich in Ihre Augen sehe, sehe ich den Mond und die Sterne. "

I "Quando guardo nei tuoi occhi vedo la luna e le stelle."

E "Cuando te miro a los ojos, veo la luna y las estrellas."

P "Quando olho para os teus olhos vejo a lua e as estrelas."

S "När jag ser in i dina ögon ser jag månen och stjärnorna."

Romantic...

GB "Are you lost? Paradise is a long way from here."

F «Vous êtes perdu ? Le Paradis est loin d'ici. »

D „Haben Sie sich verlaufen ? Ich dachte das Paradies wäre weit weg von hier. "

I "Ti sei perso? Il paradiso è molto distante da qui."

E "¿Estás perdido? El paraíso está muy lejos de aquí."

P "Estás perdido? O paraíso fica muito longe daqui."

S "Har du gått vilse, eller? Paradiset ligger långt härifrån."

Romantic...

GB "I'm sorry, I seem to have dropped my heart at your feet."

F « Désolée, je crois que mon cœur est tombé à vos pieds. »

D „Verzeihung, ich glaube ich habe mein Herz auf Ihren Fuß fallenlassen."

I "Mi perdoni, ma credo di essere caduta ai suoi piedi."

E "Lo siento. Parece que se me ha caído el corazón a tus pies."

P "Desculpe, parece-me que deixei cair o meu coração aos seus pés."

S "Jag är ledsen men jag tror att jag har tappat mitt hjärta vid dina fötter."

Romantic...

GB "I'm sure you didn't mean to turn me on looking like that, but it's too late"

F «Je suis certaine que tu ne voulais pas m'exciter à ce point mais c'est trop tard maintenant !»

D „Ich bin sicher, dass Sie mich nicht so ansehen wollten. Macht nichts, jetzt ist es sowieso zu spät."

I "Sono sicura che non era nelle tue intenzioni di farmi perdere la testa in questo modo, ma ormai è troppo tardi!"

E "Estoy segura de que no pretendías encenderme con ese cuerpo serrano, pero ahora es demasiado tarde."

P "Tenho a certeza de que você não queria que eu me virasse ao fitar-me dessa maneira, mas agora é demasiado tarde."

S "Jag är säker på att det inte var din avsikt att tända mig, men det är för sent att komma med ursäkter nu!"

Romantic...

GB "If you walk away now, I'll die with a broken heart."

F « Si tu pars maintenant, j'en mourrai le cœur brisé. »

D „Wenn Sie jetzt weggehen, werde ich an gebrochenem Herzen sterben."

I "Se ora te ne vai, avrò il cuore spezzato."

E "Si te vas ahora, moriré con el corazón roto."

P "Se te fores embora agora, morrerei com o coração partido."

S "Om du går din väg nu, kommer jag att dö med ett krossat hjärta."

Romantic...

GB "What time do you have to be back in heaven?"

F « A quelle heure dois-tu retourner au paradis ? »

D „Wann müssen Sie wieder im Himmel sein ? "

I "A che ora devi rientrare in paradiso?"

E "¿A qué hora tienes que estar de vuelta en el cielo?"

P "A que horas tens que regressar ao céu?"

S "Hur dags måste du vara tillbaka i himlen?"

Romantic...

GB "Where have you been all my life?"

F « Où était tu passé pendant toute ma vie ? »

D „Wo waren Sie mein ganzes Leben lang ? "

I "Dove sei stato fino adesso nella mia vita?"

E "¿Dónde has estado toda mi vida?"

P "Onde é que estiveste durante toda a minha vida?"

S "Var har du varit i hela mitt liv?"

Sexy...

Sexy...

GB "Do you like short love affairs? I hate them. I've got all weekend."

F « Tu aimes les histoires d'amour courtes ? Je les déteste. J'ai tout le week-end devant moi. »

D „Mögen Sie kurze Affären? Ich hasse sie, zum Glück habe ich das ganze Wochenende Zeit."

I "Ti piacciono le relazioni brevi? Io le odio. Ho tutto il fine settimana a disposizione."

E "¿Te van los rollos de una noche? Yo los odio. Tengo todo el fin de semana."

P "Gostas de casos amorosos curtos? Eu detesto-os. Tenho todo o fim de semana."

S "Gillar du korta kärleksaffärer? Jag hatar dem. Jag har hela helgen på mig."

Sexy...

GB "I don't want to sleep with you. I'm going to keep you up all night."

F « Je ne veux pas dormir avec toi. Je vais te maintenir éveillé toute la nuit. »

D „ Ich möchte nicht mit Ihnen schlafen, ich möchte Sie die ganze Nacht wachhalten. "

I "Non voglio dormire con te. Ho intenzione di tenerti sveglio tutta la notte."

E "No quiero dormir contigo. Voy a tenerte despierto toda la noche."

P "Não quero dormir contigo. Vou manter-te acordado toda a noite."

S "Jag vill inte sova med dig. Jag tänker hålla dig vaken hela natten."

Sexy...

GB "I don't love you, but I could!"

F «Je ne t'aime pas, mais je pourrais!»

D „Ich liebe Sie nicht, aber ich könnte mich dazu durchringen."

I "Non ti amo, ma potrei!"

E "No te quiero, pero podría."

P "Não te amo, mas bem que poderia."

S "Jag älskar dig inte, men jag skulle kunna!"

Sexy...

GB "I'm new in town, could I get directions to your place?"

F « Je suis nouvelle dans cette ville, quelle est la route pour aller chez toi ? »

D „ Ich bin neu in dieser Stadt, in welcher Richtung wohnen Sie ? "

I "Sono nuova da queste parti, potresti dirmi come ci arrivo a casa tua?"

E "Soy nueva en la ciudad. ¿Podrías indicarme el camino a tu casa?"

P "Sou nova na cidade, como é que se vai para a tua casa?"

S "Jag är ny här i stan, kan du beskriva vägen hem till dig?"

Sexy...

GB "That shirt looks great on you, but as a matter of fact, so would I."

F « Cette chemise te va très bien mais en fait moi aussi je t'irais très bien. »

D „ Das Hemd steht Ihnen gut, aber, um ehrlich zu sein, das würde ich auch. "

I "Quella camicia ti sta proprio bene addosso, ma a dire il vero, anch'io."

E "Esta camisa te sienta de maravilla, aunque en realidad, también me sentaría bien a mí."

P "Essa camisa fica-te bem, mas na verdade, também eu."

S "Den skjortan är jättesexig på dig men det skulle faktiskt jag också vara."

Sexy...

GB "Have you ever played nude leap-frog?"

F « Tu as déjà joué tout nu à saute mouton? »

D „ Haben Sie schon einmal nackt Frosch gespielt ? "

I "Hai mai fatto il gioco della cavallina nudo?"

E "¿Has jugado alguna vez al potro desnudo?"

P "Alguma vez saltaste ao eixo nu?"

S "Har du någonsin hoppat bock naken?"

Sexy...

GB "If you buy me a drink, I promise I'll swallow!"

F « Si tu m'offre un verre, je promets d'avaler ! »

D „Wenn Sie mir einen ausgeben, verspreche ich zu schlucken."

I "Se mi offri da bere, ti prometto che ingoio!"

E "Si me invitas a una copa, te prometo que tragaré."

P "Se me ofereceres uma bebida, prometo-te que a engulo!"

S "Om du bjuder mig på en drink så lovar jag att svälja!"

Sexy...

GB "Sex is a killer... want to die happy?"

F « L'amour tue... tu veux mourir heureux ? »

D „ Sex ist ein Killer... möchten Sie glücklich sterben ? "

I "Il sesso uccide... vuoi morire felice?"

E "El sexo mata... ¿quieres morir feliz?"

P "O sexo é um assassino... queres morrer feliz?"

S "Sex kan döda...vill du dö lycklig?"

Sexy...

GB "Do you know how to use a whip?"

F « Tu sais utiliser un fouet ? »

D „Wissen Sie, wie man eine Peitsche benutzt ? "

I "Sai usare la frusta?"

E "¿Sabes como utilizar un látigo?"

P "Sabes como usar um chicote?"

S "Vet du hur man använder en piska?"

Sexy...

GB "Do you want to be naked?"

F « Tu veux bien être à nu ? »

D „Möchten Sie sich ausziehen ? "

I "Vuoi essere nudo?"

E "¿Quieres estar desnudo?"

P "Queres ficar nu?"

S "Vill du vara naken?"

Sexy...

GB "Hi, I'm not trying to pressure you, 1 don't want to have sex without mutual consent. By the way, you have my consent."

F « Salut ! Je ne te presse pas, je ne couche pas sans consentement mutuel. Au fait, tu as mon consentement. »

D „ Hallo, ich möchte Sie ja nicht unter Druck setzen, aber ich will auch keinen Sex ohne beidseitige Zustimmung. Wo wir gerade davon sprechen, ich stimme zu. "

I "Ciao, non sto cercando di metterti pressione e non mi piace fare l'amore senza consenso. A proposito, hai il mio consenso."

E "Hola. No te estoy presionando, no quiero acostarme contigo sin mutuo acuerdo. A propósito, tienes mi consentimiento."

P "Olá, não estou a tentar pressionar-te, não quero fazer amor sem consentimento mútuo. Entretanto, tens o meu consentimento."

S "Hej, jag försöker att inte pressa dig, jag vill inte ha sex utan ditt tillstånd. Förresten, du har mitt."

Sexy...

GB "How about you and I go back to my place and get me out of these wet clothes?"

F « Ça te dit de rentrer chez moi et de me retirer ces vêtements mouillés ? »

D „Vielleicht sollten wir beide zu mir nach Hause gehen, damit ich aus diesen nassen Sachen komme."

I "Cosa ne dici se andiamo a casa mia e io mi tolgo di dosso questo vestito bagnato?"

E "¿Qué te parece si nos vamos a mi casa y me quitas esta ropa húmeda?"

P "Que tal eu e tu irmos para minha casa e eu livrar-me destas roupas molhadas?"

S "Vad sägs om att du och jag åker hem till mig och ser till att jag kommer ur de här våta kläderna?"

Sexy...

GB "I'd like to name a multiple orgasm after you."

F « Je voudrais donner ton nom à un orgasme multiple. »

D „Ich würde gern einen multiplen Orgasmus nach Ihnen nennen."

I "Mi piacerebbe battezzare un orgasmo multiplo col tuo nome."

E "Me gustaría ponerle tu nombre a un orgasmo múltiple."

P "Gostaria de dar o teu nome a um orgasmo múltiplo."

S "Jag skulle vilja uppkalla en multipel orgasm efter dig."

Sexy...

GB "Lie down. I think I love you."

F « Couche toi. Je crois que je t'aime. »

D „ Legen Sie sich hin, ich glaube, ich liebe Sie. "

I "Sdraiati. Credo di amarti."

E "Échate. Creo que te quiero."

P "Deita-te. Acho que te amo."

S "Lägg dig ner. Jag tror att jag älskar dig."

Sexy...

GB "Nice waistcoat. Can I wear it when I fix breakfast tomorrow?"

F « Joli gilet. Je pourrais le mettre quand je préparerai le petit déjeuner demain matin ? »

D „ Schöne Weste – Kann ich sie morgen früh tragen, wenn ich Frühstück mache ? "

I "Bel gilè. Posso mettermelo domani mattina mentre ti preparo la colazione?"

E "Bonito chaleco. ¿Puedo ponérmelo mañana mientras te preparo el desayuno?"

P "Lindo colete. Posso vesti-lo quando fizer o pequeno-almoço amanhã?"

S "Snygg tröja. Kan jag ha på mig den när jag lagar frukost i morgon?"

Sexy...

GB "That outfit would look great on my bedroom floor tomorrow morning."

F « Cette tenue fera très bien par terre dans ma chambre demain matin »

D „ Ihr Anzug würde sich morgen früh gut auf meinem Schlafzimmerfussboden machen. "

I "Quel completo che indossi starà benissimo sul pavimento della mia camera da letto domani mattina."

E "Esta ropa quedaría fantástica en el suelo de mi habitación mañana por la mañana."

P "Essa indumentária vai ficar óptima no chão do meu quarto amanhã de manhã."

S "Dina kläder skulle vara snygga på mitt sovrumsgolv i morgon."

Sexy...

GB "You remind me of a man I slept with in a past life."

F « Tu me rappelle un homme avec qui j'ai couché dans un vie antérieure. »

D „ Sie erinnern mich an einen Mann, mit dem ich in einen anderen Leben geschlafen habe. "

I "Mi ricordi tanto un uomo con cui ho fatto l'amore in una mia vita precedente."

E "Me recuerdas a un hombre con quien me acosté en una vida anterior."

P "Você recorda-me um homem com quem dormi numa d minhas vidas anteriores."

S "Du påminner mig om en man jag älskade med i mitt förra liv."

Sexy...

GB "Your legs are gorgeous – they'd make a wonderful necklace."

F « Tes jambes sont superbes. Elle feraient un magnifique collier. »

D „ Tolle Beine, die würden mir als Halskette gut stehen. "

I "Hai delle gambe stupende... possono diventare una collana meravigliosa."

E "Tienes unas piernas imponentes. Serían un magnífico collar."

P "As tuas pernas são soberbas – fariam um belo colar!"

S "Dina ben är härliga – de skulle se bra ut som halsband."

Sexy...

GB "You look better and better each day... and tonight, you look like tomorrow morning!"

F «Tu es de plus en plus beau jour après jour et ce soir tu seras comme demain matin »

D „ Sie sehen jeden Tag besser aus ... und heute Nacht sehen Sie schon aus wie morgen früh. "

I "Migliori sempre di più giorno dopo giorno... e notte dopo notte, e sembri proprio come domani mattina!"

E "Estás más guapo cada día... y esta noche estás tan guapo como mañana por la mañana."

P "Estás cada dia melhor... e esta noite, pareces-te com amanhã de manhã."

S "Du blir bättre och bättre dag för dag...och i kväll är du som i morgon!"

Sexy...

GB "Hi, my name's coffee – I'll keep you up all night!"

F « Salut, je m'appelle café et je vais t'empêcher de dormir cette nuit ! »

D „Hallo, mein Name ist Kaffee – ich halte Sie die ganze Nacht wach."

I "Ciao, mi chiamo caffè – ti terrò sveglio tutta la notte!"

E "Hola. Me llamo café. Te tendré despierto toda la noche."

P "Olá, o meu nome é café – vou manter-te acordado toda a noite!"

S "Hej, jag har kaffe hemma – men det är inte det som kommer att hålla dig vaken hela natten!"

Sexy...

GB "I bet you look great naked."

F « Je parie que tu es superbe tout nu. »

D „Ich wette, dass Sie nackt toll aussehen ."

I "Scommetto che sei fantastico nudo."

E "Apuesto a que estás magnífico desnudo."

P "Aposto que ficas bem nu."

S "Jag är säker på att du är jättesnygg naken."

Sexy...

GB "I need to take a shower. Want to come?"

F « J'ai besoin de prendre une douche, tu veux venir ? »

D „Ich muss duschen. Wollen Sie mitkommen ? "

I "Devo fare una doccia. Vuoi venire?"

E "Necesito una ducha. ¿Te apuntas?"

P "Preciso de tomar um duche. Quer vir?"

S "Jag måste ta en dusch. Vill du vara med?"

Sexy...

GB "Let's go back to my place and get something straightened out."

F « Rentrons chez moi et on va redresser la situation. »

D „ Gehen wir zu mir und klären das Ganze. "

I "Andiamo a casa mia e mettiamo a nudo la situazione."

E "Vamos a mi casa y resolvamos algo."

P "Vamos até minha casa fazer qualquer coisa na horizontal."

S "Låt oss åka hem till mig och räta ut saken."

Sexy...

GB "That's a really nice smile you've got, shame it's not all you are wearing."

F « J'adore ton sourire, dommage que ce ne soit pas tout ce que tu portes. »

D „ Sie haben ein nettes Lächeln, schade dass das nicht das Einzige ist, was Sie tragen. "

I "Hai proprio un sorriso meraviglioso, peccato che sia l'unica cosa che posso ammirare di te al momento."

E "Realmente tienes una sonrisa preciosa, lástima que no sea lo único que llevas puesto."

P "Você tem realmente um lindo sorriso, é pena que não seja a única coisa que tenha vestido."

S "Ditt leende klär dig, synd att det inte är det enda som gör det."

Sexy...

GB "Your body is over 90% water, and I'm really thirsty."

F «Votre corps est constitué de 90 % d'eau, et j'ai vraiment soif.»

D „Ihr Körper besteht aus mehr als 90 % Wasser und ich habe großen Durst."

I "90% del tuo corpo è acqua, e io ho tanta sete!"

E "Más del 90% de tu cuerpo es agua, y yo tengo una sed que me muero."

P "O teu corpo tem mais de 90% de água e estou cheio de sede."

S "Din kropp innehåller över 90% vatten och jag är väldig törstig."

Sexy...

GB "I don't bite... unless you ask me to."

F « Je ne mords pas...à moins que vous ne me le demandiez. »

D „ Ich beiße nicht... es sei denn Sie bitten mich darum. "

I "Non mordo ... a meno che tu lo desideri."

E "No muerdo... a menos que me lo pidas."

P "Eu não mordo... A menos que mo peças."

"Jag bits inte...såvida du inte ber mig."

Sexy...

GB "Picture this: You, me, a bubble bath, a bottle of champagne..."

F « Imaginez : Vous, moi, un bain moussant, une bouteille de champagne... »

D „ Stellen Sie sich das mal vor : Sie, ich, ein Schaumbad, eine Flasche Sekt... "

I "Immaginati noi due, una vasca piena di bolle di sapone, una bottiglia di champagne ..."

E "Imagínate esto: Tú, yo, un baño de burbujas, una botell de champaña..."

P "Imagine o seguinte. Você, eu, um banho de espuma, uma garrafa de champanhe..."

S "Föreställ dig det här: Du, jag, ett bubbelbad, en flaska champagne..."